Success guides

Intermediate 2
Computing

✗ Richard Ellis ✗

Contents

Unit 1 – The Intermediate 2 Course

Unit 2 – Computer systems

Unit 3 – Software development

Unit 4 – Artificial intelligence

Unit 5 – Computer networking

Unit 6 – Multimedia technology

Unit 7 – Coursework task

Course outline and assessment

Syllabus

The Intermediate 2 course consists of three units. Unit 1 and unit 2 are mandatory and unit 3 is chosen from three optional units.

Compulsory units	Optional units (one from these three)
Computer Systems	Artificial Intelligence
Software Development	Computer Networking
	Multimedia Technology

This book presents the content of all five units in a more compact and digestible form than a full-blown textbook. However, care has been taken to make sure that each topic has been covered in sufficient depth to give the candidate a strong position from which to tackle the exam.

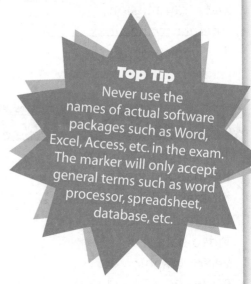

Top Tip
Never use the names of actual software packages such as Word, Excel, Access, etc. in the exam. The marker will only accept general terms such as word processor, spreadsheet, database, etc.

Assessment

Your grade for this course is determined by an exam and a coursework task. The exam has 70 marks and the coursework task has 30 marks. The coursework task changes every year and will be covered in some detail in the last topic in this book.

Unit assessment

In addition, each unit has NAB (National Assessment Bank) tests which must be passed for you to complete the course. However, these tests do not contribute towards your overall grade for the course and are intended to be tests of a basic level of understanding.

Each unit has a multiple-choice theory test and a practical checklist of skills that you have to demonstrate to your teacher.

The multiple-choice tests have a pass mark of 12 out of 20. To demonstrate the practical skills, your teacher will give you short practical tasks to perform. If you fail an assessment then you have a second chance.

The exam

The exam lasts for 1 hour 30 minutes and has a total of 70 marks. Try to pace yourself through the exam. Try to find a balance between finishing too early because you have not written answers with enough depth and explanation, and rushing to finish and not completing the exam. Look at the clock every 15 minutes and gauge your progress.

Try to write neatly; this will keep the marker in a better mood than if he/she has to struggle to decipher your answers.

The exam is split up into three sections as described below.

Section 1

This section is made up of short response questions based on the two compulsory units 'Computer Systems' and 'Software Development'.
Total marks 15.

Section 2

This section is made up of extended response questions based on the two compulsory units 'Computer Systems' and 'Software development'.
Total marks 30.

Section 3

This section is made up of extended response questions based on the three optional units 'Artificial Intelligence', 'Computer networking' and 'Multimedia Systems'.

You answer only one of these three optional units!

Total marks 25.

Top Tip
Each year an alarmingly high number of pupils attempt to answer the questions in all three optional units in the exam. **Remember**: just answer the questions from **one** of the three optional units which your own school has covered.

Look up the SQA website, which has useful information on the exam at www.sqa.org.uk. This site has information on the exam timetable, reviews of previous exams, appeals procedures, etc.

Data representation 1

Binary code

A computer is a two state electronic device which can represent the states of current ON and current OFF. The binary number system has two digits, 1 (current ON) and 0 (current OFF), and is used to represent data and instructions in a computer.

Advantages of using binary

Computers use the binary number system and not the decimal number system for several reasons.

1. It is a simple two state system where ON is represented by a 1 and OFF is represented by a 0.

2. Arithmetic calculations are simpler since there are fewer combinations of 1s and 0s. For example, there are only four rules for addition: 0 + 0, 1 + 0, 0 + 1 and 1 + 1, whereas the decimal system would require 100 rules.

3. It is easier to represent two states physically on backing storage devices. For example, pits and lands can be used to represent 1s and 0s on a CD-ROM.

101100010
01100010010

Top Tip
It is a common mistake to use 1,000 for Kb instead of 1,024 and 1,000,000 for Mb instead of 1,048,576, etc.

Units

Units of capacity in computing are based upon powers of 2 because computers work in binary.

The following units are used to describe file sizes and storage capacities on a computer system.

A Bit is a binary digit (1 or 0).

A Byte is a group of 8 bits.

A Kilobyte (Kb) is 1,024 bytes, which is 2^{10} bytes.

A Megabyte (Mb) is 1,048,576 bytes, which is 2^{20} bytes.

A Gigabyte (Gb) is 1,073,741,824 bytes, which is 2^{30} bytes.

A Terabyte (Tb) is 1,099,511,627,776 bytes, which is 2^{40} bytes.

Numbers

Whole numbers are stored in a computer in binary. The binary system (base 2) uses powers of 2 as opposed to the decimal number system (base 10) which uses powers of 10. The example below shows how the number 185 is stored in binary.

128	64	32	16	8	4	2	1
1	0	1	1	1	0	0	1

$= (128 \times 1) + (64 \times 0) + (32 \times 1) + (16 \times 1) + (8 \times 1) + (4 \times 0) + (2 \times 0) + (1 \times 1)$
$= \mathbf{185}$

Floating-point representation

Floating-point numbers are made up of a decimal fraction part called the mantissa and a power part called the **exponent.**

For example, $101101101110 = \mathbf{0.1011011} \times 2^{12} = \mathbf{0.1011011} \times 2^{1100}$

Mantissa: 1011011   Exponent: 1100

Advantage

Very large and very small numbers can be represented in a few number of bits.

Disadvantage

Accuracy is lost because the mantissa is rounded off to a set number of significant figures.

Top Tip
In this course you are only required to convert 8-bit binary numbers into decimal and vice versa. You do not need to worry about larger numbers at this stage.

Quick Test

1. Give one reason why computers store data using the binary system.

2. Put the following terms in decreasing order of size. Byte, Tb, Kb, Gb, bit, Mb.

3. Convert the number 137 into 8-bit binary.

4. Describe the two components of a floating point number.

Data representation 2

Text

Text is stored on a computer system by using a unique binary code for each character. The ASCII (American Standard Code for Information Interchange) code system uses an 8 bit (1 byte) code to represent each character. For example, the ASCII codes for character 'E' and 'T' are 01000101 and 01010100 respectively.

Control characters

These are ASCII codes for characters that are not printed but do things such as control the layout of the text. Examples include the TAB and RETURN control characters.

Character set

A character set is the complete list of characters that the computer system can represent. For example, the ASCII code system can represent 128 characters made up of upper-case letters (A, B, C ... Z), lower-case letters (a, b, c ... z), digits (0, 1, 2 ... 9), mathematical and punctuation symbols (+, >, ?, ! ...) and control characters.

Top Tip

The 'space' character is not a control character, although it obviously does not print a character. Think of it as printing a blank character as opposed to not printing anything at all.

Bitmap graphics

A bitmap graphics program stores the data as a two-dimensional grid of pixels. Pixels are the tiny dots that make up the image. (The word pixel comes from the phrase 'picture element'.)

Resolution

The term 'resolution' is the number of pixels in a fixed area. High resolution is a large number of small pixels. Low resolution is a small number of large pixels. High resolution graphics give better quality than low resolution graphics but require more storage. Resolution is usually measured in dpi (dots per inch).

Bit depth

This term states the number of bits used to encode the colour of each pixel. The higher the bit depth then the higher the number of colours that can be represented.

High Resolution Graphics

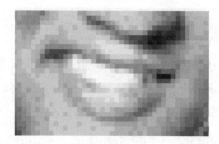

Low Resolution Graphics

Storage calculations

Each pixel in a black and white graphic can have two possible states: black or white. One bit is required to store the colour of each pixel. Black is represented by a 1 and white is represented by a 0. Therefore the number of bits required to store a black and white image is the same as the number of pixels in the graphic.

240 pixels

320 pixels

For example, the graphic shown contains 240 × 320 = 76,800 pixels.
Each pixel requires 1 bit of storage. Therefore the total storage requirement is
76,800 bits = 76,800 /8 bytes
= 9,600 bytes = 9,600/1024 Kb
= 9.4 Kb.

Quick Test

1. What do the letters ASCII stand for?

2. What is a character set?

3. Explain how a bit-mapped graphic is stored on a computer system.

4. Calculate the storage requirements in bytes for a black and white graphic that measures 560 by 400 pixels.

Answers 1. American Standard Code for Information Interchange. It is used to represent text in a computer system. **2.** A character set is the complete list of characters that a computer system can represent. **3.** A graphic is stored as a bitmap in which a binary code represents the colour of each pixel that makes up the graphic. **4.** Storage requirements = 560 × 400 bits = 224,000 bits = 224,000/8 bytes = 28,000 bytes.

Computer structure

Computer system

The diagram represents the main components of a computer system. The processor and the main memory are part of the CPU (Central Processing Unit). Input, output and backing storage devices are called peripheral devices.

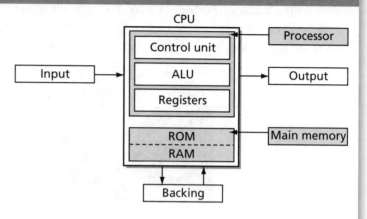

Input

Input devices such as a keyboard are used to enter data into the computer.

Output

Output devices such as a printer are used to display the results of processing.

Backing storage

Backing storage devices are used to permanently store program and data files.

Processor

The processor is the brains of the computer system and manages the execution of programs.

Purpose of a processor

The processor manages the fetching and execution of program instructions held in main memory and performs any required calculations.

Main memory

Main memory stores the programs and data that are currently being executed by the processor.

Top Tip

It is fairly common to be asked questions about this diagram in the exam such as labelling missing components, so make sure that you study it well.

Processor structure

The processor has three components:

1. Control unit

The control unit sends out signals to control the fetching and execution of program instructions held in main memory. It has electronic circuits that decode and execute the instructions.

2. ALU (Arithmetic Logic Unit)

The ALU performs arithmetic ($+$, $-$, $\times$, $/$) and logical decisions such as AND and OR.

3. Registers

These are individual storage locations on the processor chip that the processor uses to temporarily hold single items of data.

Main memory and backing storage

Main memory is located inside the CPU and is used to store the programs and data being currently executed by the processor. It is made up of RAM and ROM chips.

Backing storage devices such as a hard disc drive are attached to the CPU and are used to store program and data files permanently.

RAM and ROM

RAM (random access memory)

Instructions and data can be written to RAM. It loses its contents when the power is switched off. Programs such as Word and Excel are loaded into RAM from backing storage devices to be executed by the processor.

ROM (read only memory)

The programs and data in ROM can be read by the processor but ROM cannot be written to. It keeps its contents when the power is switched off. The contents of ROM are put there when the chip is manufactured, and cannot be changed. ROM is used to store programs important for the system such as the BIOS, which is an important part of the computer's operating system.

Top Tip

A lot of abbreviations such as ALU are used in computing. It is important that you learn what ALU, RAM, etc. stand for. For example, you should know that ALU stands for Arithmetic Logic Unit.

Quick Test

1. What is the function of a backing storage device on a computer system?

2. Name one input, one output and one backing storage device.

3. Name the three component parts of a processor.

4. What does RAM stand for?

Answers 1. A backing storage device is used to permanently hold program and data files. 2. Input: keyboard, mouse, digital camera, etc; Output: printer, screen, etc.; Backing storage: hard disc drive, USB memory stick, floppy disc, etc. 3. Control unit, ALU and registers. 4. Random Access Memory.

Types of computer and performance

Types of computer

Palmtop

This computer fits in a human hand and can be used as an electronic diary. Palmtop computers allow handwritten text to be converted into editable text using OCR (optical character recognition) software.

Smartphones incorporate the standard functions of a mobile phone and a handheld computer in one device.

Laptop

This computer is light enough to be carried around. Laptop computers are convenient for working in places such as airports and cafés. They provide the same level of functionality as a desktop computer and can run applications packages and provide Internet access.

Desktop

This computer fits comfortably on a desk. A desktop computer is popular for business and home use and provides Internet access and runs applications packages.

Mainframe

This is a very powerful and expensive computer that is used by large organisations to process and store vast amounts of data.

Embedded

This computer system is the hardware and software that forms part of a larger system.

For example, a washing machine has an embedded computer which is made up of the built-in processor and memory chips together with the program that carries out the washing machine's functions.

Top Tip
Portable is a word used to describe a computer that can be easily carried around.

Comparison of types of computer

Speed of processor

Starting with the slowest, the processor speed increases in this order: palmtop, laptop, desktop, mainframe.

Size of main memory

The amount of RAM increases in the same order as for the processing speed given above.

A palmtop computer has around 16 Mb of RAM, a laptop and desktop around 3 Gb and a mainframe can have many times more RAM than these computers.

Backing storage

The capacity increases in the same order again.

A palmtop has a backing storage capacity of around 256 Mb. Laptop and desktop computers have hard disc capacities of around 200–300 Gb and CD and DVD drives. Mainframes can have an enormous amount of backing storage.

Input and output devices

A palmtop computer uses a stylus to write on a touch sensitive screen.

A laptop computer uses a touchpad to move a pointer around the screen to select items.

A desktop computer uses a mouse instead of a touchpad, since there is a surface available on which to move the mouse.

Laptop and desktop computers have standard keyboards, LCD or TFT flat screens for their displays

Top Tip
Use the Internet to familiarise yourself with the current specification of palmtop, laptop and desktop computers.

System performance

One measure of the performance of a computer is given by the clock speed. This is a measure of how fast the processor is fetching and executing the program instructions.

A typical clock speed of a desktop or laptop computer is between 2 GHz and 3 GHz. A palmtop computer has a slower clock speed of around 300 MHz.

Quick Test

1. What input device does a laptop use instead of a mouse?

2. What is an embedded computer system?

3. Which type of computer is used to process vast amounts of information in large organisations?

4. Which of the following is a typical clock speed of a desktop computer?

   A 3 KHz; **B** 3 MHz; **C** 3 GHz; **D** 3 THz

Answers 1. Touchpad. **2.** The hardware and software that forms part of a larger system. **3.** Mainframe. **4.** C.

Peripherals 1

Comparison of input and output devices

A comparison between different input and output devices can be done using the following characteristics.

Resolution

This is the number of pixels that are captured by a device. A resolution of a digital camera is measured in megapixels, whereas the resolution of a printer is measured in dpi (dots per inch).

Capacity

This is the amount of data that the input/output device can store.

Speed of data transfer

This is how fast the data can be transferred from or to the device.

Cost

Clearly, devices can be compared by their cost.

Input devices

Keyboard

A keyboard is used to type data into a computer. This is a slow method of entering data compared to automatic methods.

Mouse

A mouse is used to move a pointer on the screen to select items.

Touchpad

A touchpad is a small pad with sensors to detect the movement and taps of a finger to move a pointer around the screen and select items.

Microphone

A microphone is used with a sound card to enter sound data into a computer.

Digital camera

A digital camera is used to input digital images into a computer. The quality of the camera resolution is measured in megapixels. A mid-range digital camera can capture around 9 megapixels.

Top Tip

There are other input and output devices, but to do well in the exam for this course just learn the features and functions of the ones mentioned in this topic.

Scanner

A scanner is used to input images on paper into a computer. The resolution of a scanner is typically 600–4,800 dpi.

Webcam

A webcam can capture video or still photos. They can be used to relay videos of places of interest over the Internet and in videoconferencing.

Output devices

Monitor

Up until recently desktop computers used a CRT (Cathode Ray Tube) for the screen display. These were bulky and heavy and have now been replaced with flat screen displays.

LCD (liquid crystal display)

This is a low-power flat screen display that is usually used on palmtop and laptop computers.

More expensive TFT (Thin Film Transistor) flat screen displays are often used on desktop computers.

Inkjet printer

An inkjet printer creates a printout by squirting tiny droplets of quick drying ink onto paper. This type of printer can incur a lot of cost in replacing the ink cartridges.

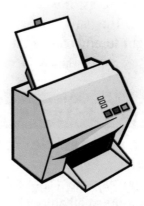

Laser printer

A laser printer creates a printout by using a laser to make an electric charge of an image on a drum which is then transferred onto paper using a powder called a toner. A laser printer produces dry printouts at a faster speed than an inkjet printer.

Loudspeakers

A loudspeaker is used with a sound card to output sound data from a computer.

Top Tip
You will prepare yourself better by studying this book in a lot of short spells rather than a few long spells.

Quick Test

1. Name **two** devices used to enter graphics into a computer system.
2. How is the resolution of a scanner measured?
3. Give **one** advantage of a laser printer over an inkjet printer.
4. Name **two** output devices.

Answers **1.** Digital camera and scanner. **2.** dpi (dots per inch) **3.** Either a laser printer produces better quality printouts or has a faster printing speed. **4.** Any two from monitor, LCD screen, printer and loudspeakers.

Peripherals 2

Comparison of backing storage devices

The characteristics of capacity and speed of data transfer are used to compare different backing storage devices. In addition, backing storage devices can be compared by their type of access.

Type of access

Sequential access is where other data has to be gone through to get to the required data. Magnetic tape has sequential access since you have to wind through other parts of the tape to get to the required data.

Direct/random access is where the read/write head can go straight to the required data. The hard disc has direct/random access since the read/write head can go straight to any part of the surface of the disc to read and write data.

Backing storage devices

Magnetic storage devices

1. **Floppy drive**

   This is a low-capacity (1.44 Mb) magnetic storage device which is useful for backing up small amounts of data.

2. **Zip drive**

   This is a medium-capacity removable magnetic storage device. The capacity ranges from 100 Mb to 800 Mb.

3. **Hard drive**

   This a high-capacity (100 Gb to 1 Tb) magnetic storage device. A hard drive has a much faster data transfer rate than both floppy drives and zip drives.

4. **Magnetic tape drive**

   This is a slow-access, fairly high-capacity magnetic backing storage device.

Optical storage devices

Optical storage devices use laser light to read and write data:

1. **CD-ROM (Compact Disc Read Only Memory)**

   The data is put on the disc at manufacture, after which it can be read but not written to. The capacity of a CD-ROM is 700 Mb and the speed of reading is given by a number such as 40X, which is a multiple of 150 Kilobits per second, so the speed is 40 × 150 = 6,000 Kb per second.

2. **CD-R (Compact Disc Recordable)**

   This optical disc allows data to written to it but only once. The speed of reading and writing is given by two numbers such as READ 52X, WRITE 40X.

3. CD-RW (Compact Disc Rewriteable)
This optical disc can be read and written to over and over again. The speed of writing, rewriting and reading is given by three numbers such as WRITING 52X, REWRITE 40X, READING 48X

4. DVD-ROM (Digital Versatile Disc Read Only Memory)
This is a high capacity optical disc (4.7 Gb) with a faster data transfer rate than a CD-ROM. Rewritable DVD discs are also available.

Top Tip
Look up the cost of peripheral devices using newspaper adverts and the Internet.

Interface

An interface is used to connect a peripheral device to the CPU and to compensate for the differences in how they operate.

Differences in speed

The processor operates at a much higher speed than peripheral devices. The interface has to compensate for these differences.

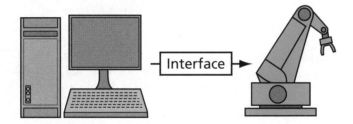

Interface

Data conversion

Data may be required to be converted from one format to another. For example, changing analogue data to digital data or changing voltage levels.

Temporary data storage

Data may be required to be stored temporarily in an area of memory called a buffer until the device is ready to transfer it.

Top Tip
Learn the storage capacities of backing storage devices such as a floppy disc, CD and DVD.

Quick Test

1. Name **one** optical backing storage device.

2. Put these backing storage devices in increasing order of capacity: hard drive, floppy drive, zip drive.

3. Name **two** characteristics that can be used to compare a hard drive and a magnetic drive.

4. What is an interface?

Answers: 1. CD drive or DVD drive. **2.** Floppy drive, zip drive, hard drive. **3.** Any two from type of access, capacity, speed of data transfer and cost. **4.** A connection between a peripheral and the CPU to compensate for differences in their speed and operation.

17

Networking 1

LANs, WANs and the Internet

A computer network is where two or more computers are linked together so that they can communicate with each other and share resources. However, linking computers together makes them more vulnerable to hacking and virus attacks.

LAN (local area network)

A LAN is a computer network that covers a small area such as a room or a building.

1. Transmission media

The transmission media used to transfer data between the computers is typically twisted wire pair, coaxial cable, copper cable, optical fibres and wireless connections.

2. Bandwidth

This is the speed of transmission and is typically between 10 and 100 Mbps.

3. Function

A LAN is used to share files, to use email for improved communications and to share hardware devices such as printers.

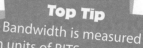

Top Tip
Bandwidth is measured in units of BITS per second not bytes per second. Kbps means 1,024 bits per second and Mbps means 1.048,576 bits per second.

WAN (wide area network)

A WAN is a computer network that covers a large area such as a city or a country.

1. Transmission Media

A WAN uses telecommunication links to connect the computers.

2. Bandwidth

Dial-up modem connections have a maximum speed of 56 Kbps but now high-speed broadband connections provide speeds of 10 Mbps.

3. Function

A WAN can be used to allow global communication through emails, to transfer files and for video conferencing.

The Internet

The Internet is a global network of individual computers and networks.

1. Transmission media

The Internet uses transmission media which include public telephone lines and wireless connections.

2. Bandwidth

Broadband connections offer around 10 Mbps.

3. Function

The Internet can be used to search for information, to buy and sell goods, to download software, etc.

Client server network

A client server network has two types of computers called clients and servers.

Client

A client is a workstation computer that accesses the network resources provided by the servers.

Server

A server is a powerful computer that provides a network resource. A file server stores and manages access to application software and the network user's files. A print server provides printing on the network by managing a queue of print requests.

Email

Email address

An email address is of the form BugsBunny@hotmail.com, where 'BugsBunny' identifies an individual and 'hotmail.com' is the server that provides the email service.

Sending

This involves entering the recipient's email address, a subject such as 'Holidays' and the message text.

Reading

This involves logging in to your account and opening your inbox.

Replying

Emails have a reply option that allows a message to be replied to without entering the email address.

Setting up an address book

Addresses of people that are sent email regularly can be stored.

Setting up mailing lists

Emails can be sent to a group of people at the same time.

Setting up folders

Emails can be organised by having them delivered to specific folders.

Top Tip
Explore the features of your own email account such as replying and setting up an address book.

Quick Test

1. What does WAN stand for?

2. Give one difference between a LAN and a WAN.

3. Name two types of server.

4. In the email address yogi@hotmail.com, what does 'hotmail.com' represent?

Answers 1. Wide Area Network **2.** A LAN covers a smaller area than a WAN, a WAN has a slower bandwidth than a WAN or there are fewer errors on a LAN than a WAN. **3.** file server , print server. **4.** hotmail.com is the server that processes the email.

Networking 2

See also Unit 5: Network Application 2. P. 64.

World Wide Web

The WWW (World Wide Web) is a virtually limitless amount of multimedia information stored on websites on server computers on the Internet. This information can be accessed by entering the address of the website into a browser or using a search engine with appropriate keywords.

Web page

A website is a collection of web pages with hyperlinks between them. Web pages contain multimedia information in the form of text, graphics, video and sound. For example, the BBC website (www.bbc.co.uk) has a home page from where the user can follow links to TV, Sport, News, etc.

Hyperlink

This is a piece of coloured text or an image which, when clicked on, provides a link to another web page.

Browser

This is a program that displays web pages and navigates between them. The most used browser is Internet Explorer.

Search engine

A search engine is a program that finds websites matching keywords entered by the user. If the URL of a web page is not known, a search engine can be used to find the site and other relevant sites by entering suitable keywords. For example, websites about the weather in Paris could be searched for with keywords such as: Paris, forecast, weather and so on.

Google and Yahoo are currently the most frequently used search engines.

> **Top Tip**
> It is better to use the term 'search engine' rather than a specific search engine such as 'Google' when answering questions in the exam.

Economic factors

Several economic factors have led to the development of computer networks:

1. The falling costs of telecommunications technologies and services.
2. Shared access to expensive equipment such as colour laser printers and high-capacity hard disc drives.
3. The global spread of organisations such as international companies requires networks to operate their business.
4. The demand for up-to-date information.

The law

Computer Misuse Act

This act makes hacking into confidential information and the sending of viruses illegal.

Data Protection Act

This act protects the right of individuals in society to ensure that data held on them by organisations such as banks, the National Health Service and sports clubs is used appropriately.

The **data subject** is the person whose data is being held.

The **data users** are the people in the organisation who use the data.

Requirements of this act include:

1. The organisation holding the data must register with the data protection registrar.
2. The data subject has a right to see what data is held about him/her with the exception of the police and national security organisations.
3. Mistakes in the data must be amended.
4. The data must be made secure.
5. Data should be deleted when it is no longer required.

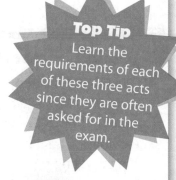

Top Tip
Learn the requirements of each of these three acts since they are often asked for in the exam.

Copyright, Designs and Patents Act

This act makes it illegal to make pirate copies of items such as software, music and literature without permission from the people who produced these items.

Quick Test

1. What is a browser?
2. Name a search engine.
3. Give an example of a piece of expensive equipment that can be shared on a computer network.
4. Which Act protects information held on computer databases about individuals in society?

Answers 1. A program that displays web pages and is used to surf the Internet. 2. Google, Ask Jeeves, etc. 3. Hard disc drive, laser printer, scanner, etc. 4. The Data Protection Act.

Operating systems, application programs and viruses

Operating systems

An operating system is a large program that manages the hardware and software of a computer system.

Examples of tasks carried out by an operating system:

1. Providing a human–computer interface (HCI) for the user to interact with the operating system.

2. Saving and loading files on disc.

3. Performing input and output with peripherals.

4. Managing the loading and execution of programs.

5. Error reporting.

Examples of operating systems are Windows Vista, Mac OS and LINUX.

Application programs

An operating system manages the computer system itself whereas an application program is a piece of software that performs a useful task for the computer user. Examples of application programs are word processing, graphics and stock control.

Standard file formats

Files can be saved in a standard file format so that they will be recognised by other computer programs. This makes it easier to transfer data from one program to another.

Standard file formats exist for Text, Sound, Graphics and Video files.

Standard file formats for text

1. ASCII (American Standard Code for Information Interchange)

This file format only stores information about which characters are in the document and does not store formatting information.

2. Text

This file format is virtually the same as ASCII but can contain some control characters such as RETURN.

3. RTF (Rich Text Format)

This file format contains information about the characters and also formatting information such as font, font size and styles such as bold and underline.

Top Tip
The RTF file format takes up more storage than ASCII since it stores extra text formatting information.

Objects and operations

Word processing, spreadsheet, database and graphics packages can be viewed as a collection of objects and a collection of the operations or actions that can be performed on those objects.

Word Processing	Object	Operations
	Word	Insert, Delete, Edit, Copy, Spellcheck, etc.
	Page	Insert footer, Change margins, etc.
	Document	Save, Open, Print, etc.

Spreadsheet	Object	Operations
	Cell	Insert text, Change border, etc.
	Row	Insert, Delete, Alter width, etc.
	Chart	Create, Resize, Format, etc.

Database	Object	Operations
	Field	Insert field, Delete field, Edit text, etc.
	Record	Insert, Delete, Amend, etc.
	File	Search, Sort, Print, etc.

Graphics	Object	Operations
	Line	Delete, Format, Bring to front, etc.
	Rectangle	Insert, Copy, Format, etc.
	Selection	Resize, Rotate, Flip vertically, etc.

Viruses

A virus is a program that causes harm to a computer system. It can replicate itself and spread to other computers. It can attach itself to an application program, system files or data files.

The following are the symptoms of a computer which is infected by a virus:

1. Displaying unwanted messages.
2. Unusual visual/sound effects.
3. Unexpected reboot of the computer.
4. The unwanted generation of emails.

A virus can spread from computer to computer through swapping floppy discs or CDs. A computer can become infected through visiting 'fun' websites or from email attachments which can contain viruses.

Anti-virus software detects and removes viruses.

Top Tip
Anti-virus software must be regularly updated since new viruses are appearing all the time.

Quick Test

1. Name a commercially available operating system.
2. Give an example of an application program.
3. What is the difference between ASCII and RTF standard file formats?
4. Give an example of a symptom of a virus infestation.

Answers 1. Windows Vista, Mac OS, LINUX, etc. **2.** Word processing, spreadsheet, database, graphics, etc. **3.** ASCII only stores the characters but RTF also stores text formatting information such as font, styles etc. **4.** Unwanted messages, unwanted generation of emails, unusual visual/sound effects, unexpected reboot.

Test your progress

Questions

1. How many bits are there in a byte?
2. Write the number 198 in binary.
3. How does a computer system store very large and very small numbers?
4. How is text stored in a computer system?
5. Calculate the storage requirements of the following black and white bitmap graphic.

640 pixels

480 pixels

6. What is a processor register?
7. Give one difference between RAM and ROM.
8. What units would be used to measure the capacity of a hard disc drive?
9. What type of access does a magnetic tape use?
10. Give an example of data conversion that the interface between the processor and a peripheral device might perform.
11. Give one disadvantage of a computer network.
12. What is a hyperlink in a web page?
13. Give two activities made illegal by the Computer Misuse Act.
14. Which of these tasks is NOT performed by an operating system?

    A: Copying a file from one disc to another.

    B: Spellchecking a document.

    C: Inputting data from a scanner.

    D: Formatting a disc.

15. Wendy works as a journalist for a newspaper in New York. The editor of the newspaper insists that Wendy sends in her articles in RTF file format in email attachments.

    Explain why the editor would want the files in RTF format.

16. Rosaleen works from home as an advertising contractor for a fashion magazine. She installed anti-virus software on her computer when she bought it 10 months ago. Recently she has started to notice signs of virus infection such as irritating messages appearing at random on her screen.

    How can Rosaleen's computer have become infected if it has anti-virus software installed?

Answers

1. 8.
2. 11000110
3. It uses floating point numbers which have a mantissa and an exponent part.
4. Each character is stored in an ASCII code using 8 bits.
5. The graphic contains 640 × 480 = 307,200 pixels.

   Each pixel requires 1 bit of storage.

   Therefore the total storage requirements = 307,200 bits = 307,200/8 bytes = 38,400 bytes.
6. A register is an individual storage location on the processor chip that the processor uses to temporarily hold single items of data.
7. Either

   RAM loses its contents when the power is switched off but ROM does not.

   Or

   The contents of RAM can be written to and changed but ROM cannot.
8. Gigabytes.
9. Sequential access.
10. Analogue to digital conversion or conversion of voltage levels.
11. Computer viruses can spread more easily over a network than stand-alone machines or, a computer network is open to hackers.
12. A hyperlink is a piece of coloured text or graphic that when clicked provides a link to another webpage or website.
13. Sending viruses and hacking into confidential information.
14. **B:** Spellchecking a document.
15. RTF is a standard file format for text that the software used to make up the newspaper from the journalists' articles will be able to open.
16. New viruses are appearing all the time so anti-virus software must be regularly updated.

How did you score

Number of answers correct:

0–6: Not very good. You need to go back and learn this topic.

7–9: Reasonable. You know some of the work but look over before moving on.

10–13: Good. You should move on but go back later and consolidate your knowledge.

14–16: Excellent. You have mastered this topic and can move on.

Software development process – the stages

Introduction

The development of a software project proceeds through 7 stages. The stages are analysis, design, implementation, testing, documentation, evaluation and maintenance. An overview of these stages will be given here but more detailed descriptions will be given later in this book.

Top Tip

Learn the 7 stages of the software development process and the order in which they come.

Analysis

The development of a project starts with an examination of the existing system and meetings with the clients to establish their needs. This stage is important in order to make sure that the software meets the requirements of the client and to have a thorough and detailed description of the problem.

Design

At this stage structure charts are used to design the structure of the program, that is, how the program is to be broken up into more manageable chunks. Also, pseudocode is used to describe the detailed logic of the program code.

Implementation

At this stage the design is turned into a program in a chosen language. In a large project there may be a team of programmers who will be allocated parts of the program to write.

Top Tip

Ask your teacher for extra exam-style questions to do in preparation for the exam.

Testing

Testing is performed to locate and remove errors. Test data is chosen to test the software as thoroughly as possible.

Documentation

Once the program has been written and fully tested documentation is produced. This includes a user guide, to help the users by describing and explaining the features of the software, and a technical guide to support the technical staff in the maintenance of the software.

Evaluation

The completed software project will be judged against a checklist of criteria to evaluate how good or bad it is. This is an essential process to make sure that the software has met the requirements of the client.

For example: 'Does the program have a user friendly human–computer interface that can be understood by the client after two days of training?'

Maintenance

The software development process does not end with the completion of the project. At some point in the future the software could well require to be modified to remove errors that were previously undetected. Often maintenance activities are performed to incorporate new features into the software as requested by the user or to modify the software to adapt to changes in the hardware and software environment in which it runs.

Quick Test

1. Why is the analysis stage required at the start of the software development process?

2. Which stage in the software development process comes after design?

3. Why is it that testing a program with one set of test data is not sufficient to conclude that it is free from errors?

4. Give one reason why a software project might require maintenance.

Analysis and design

Analysis

The software development process begins with meeting with the client to extract their needs and to find out the requirements and boundaries of the software solution. In a large project this can take months, since development cannot proceed until a clear and detailed specification of the problem is produced.

Some techniques used at the analysis stage include:

1. Interviewing the client to find out their needs.

2. Observing people at work and making notes on what they do.

3. Issuing questionnaires to gather information.

4. Looking at the existing documentation that the company uses.

Design

The design stage differs from the analysis stage in that the analysis stage is concerned with WHAT the problem is but the design stage is concerned with HOW to solve the problem.

The detailed specification of the problem resulting from the analysis stage is used as a basis for the design of the solution. The design will include a plan for the structure of the program, the detailed logic of the program code and drawings of screen layouts.

Top Tip
Practise doing past exam papers for the Intermediate 2 course; this will help you prepare for the exam.

Structure diagram

A structure diagram is the most popular way of illustrating the structure of the program.

Human beings find it easier to solve a small problem than a large problem. A structure diagram is used to break down a problem step by step into smaller and smaller problems until the problems are easy to solve.

Top Tip
The process of progressively breaking down a problem into smaller and smaller chunks is called stepwise refinement.

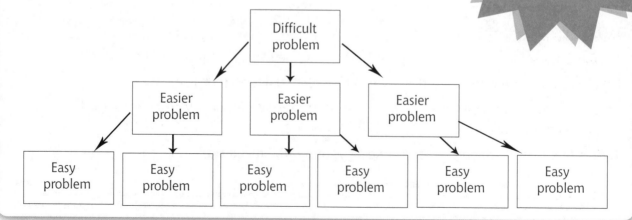

Pseudocode

Pseudocode is used to describe the detailed logic of the program code before it is written in a chosen programming language. It lies somewhere between programming code and natural language.

The advantage of pseudocode is that it can be used to describe the detailed logic of a program without having to worry about the rules of a programming language.

Example

A program enters the age of the user and then displays a message saying if the user is a child or an adult (Child = 0–17, Adult = 18 and over).

Shown below is the algorithm in pseudocode and also the program implemented in a programming language (Visual Basic)

Pseudocode

1. Get the name of the user
2. Get the age from the user
3. If the age is less than 18 then
4.   Display a message that the user is a child
5. Else
6.   Display message that the user is an adult
7. End of if

Visual Basic

```
Let Username = InputBox("Please enter your name.")
Let Age = InputBox("Please enter your age.")
If Age < 18 Then
      Picture1.Print Username; "you are a child."
Else
      Picture1.Print Username; "you are an adult."
End If
```

Quick Test

1. What is the purpose of the analysis stage of the software development process?
2. Give one technique used to gather information about the problem at the analysis stage.
3. What is a structure diagram?
4. Which design technique shows the detailed logic of the program code?

Answers 1. To study the problem and come up with a clear and detailed description of the requirements of the solution. 2. Interviewing the client, observation notes, questionnaires, examining existing documents, etc. 3. A structure diagram shows the breaking down of a problem into progressively smaller and smaller chunks. 4. Pseudocode.

29

Implementation and testing

Implementation

At this stage programmers write the lines of code for the software in a suitable programming language. A high-level language is usually chosen for the implementation of the software solution, but sometimes it can be preferable to use an application program such as a spreadsheet or database because they have a user interface and built-in functions already in place. This would make the development time quicker than writing code, but there would not be as much control over customisation.

The structure diagram produced at the design stage which splits the program down into small chunks called procedures can be used to allocate to different programmers.

Top Tip
You may have a textbook for this course which is several times longer than this book. However, if you learn the contents of this book it will focus your attention on what is required for the exam.

Testing

Once the program has been written, the next stage is to test the program to locate any errors so that they can be removed. It is impossible to test the program with the almost limitless number of possible inputs that a large software project can be given, but test data is used to test the program as much as is reasonably possible.

Top Tip
After the software has been tested by the software development team the final testing stage is for the software to be tested by the clients in their place of work.

Test data

There are three types of test data:

Normal

One set of test data should be chosen to test that the software gives correct results for commonplace data which falls within the expected range of values.

Extreme

One set of test data should be chosen to see if the software can handle data on the boundaries of valid data.

Exceptional

One set of test data should be chosen for extreme cases in order to test that the software can cope with unexpected data without crashing.

Example of choosing test data

A program prompts the user to enter how many grandparents they have that are still living as a number from 0 to 4. A procedure is used to enter and validate the number of grandparents. The following are examples of normal, extreme and exceptional data that could be used to test the subroutine.

Normal Test Data	Number of grandparents	3, 1, 2
Extreme Data	Number of grandparents	0, 4
Exceptional Data	Number of grandparents	−1, 7, 'Three', 'Yes'

Quick Test

1. What documentation produced at the design stage can a programmer use to help him or her write the detailed logic of the lines of code of a program?

2. Which stage in the software development process comes after implementation?

3. What is the purpose of the testing stage in the software development process?

4. Name three types of test data that are used to fully test software.

Answers 1. Pseudocode. **2.** Testing. **3.** The purpose of testing is to locate and remove any errors in the software. **4.** Normal, extreme and exceptional data.

Documentation, evaluation and maintenance

Documentation

Items of documentation are produced to help the users with the features of the software, and explain how to install and run it.

User guide

This can be in the form of a user manual or in electronic form. It gives instructions on how to use the features of the software and can include tutorials to give lessons.

Technical guide

This gives technical details on how to install the software and the minimum system requirements for the processor, RAM and hard disc capacity, etc.

Top Tip
Know the difference between a user guide and a technical guide and what is contained in each.

Evaluation

Once the software project has been completed it is evaluated against a set of criteria. For the purpose of this course, software is judged against the following three criteria:

1. Fitness for purpose

A program is fit for purpose if it does what it is supposed to do. The software is compared with the requirements that were agreed with the client at the analysis stage to see if it meets them.

2. User interface

The user interface is evaluated to see if it is easy for the clients to understand and use. It is judged on factors such as the consistency of menus and fonts, screen layouts, warning and error messages, online help, etc.

3. Readability

Software is readable if it is easily understood by another programmer. A program is made readable by using meaningful variable names such as StartReading rather than X, using internal commentary to explain the lines of code, using indentation and blank lines to give the program listing some structure, etc.

Top Tip
Terms like 'fit for purpose' and 'readable' have a precise meaning in this course, so learn the definitions given here. Of course, you can use your own language but don't stray too far away from these definitions.

Maintenance

Once a software project has been completed that is not the end of the matter.
There are three main reasons for this:

1. Errors that were not detected at the development stage may need to be corrected.

2. The client may ask for new features to be added to the software.

3. The software may be required to be adapted to run on a new operating system or to incorporate new hardware devices.

Quick Test

1. Name two items of documentation that are produced for a software development project.

2. What does the term 'fit for purpose' mean?

3. What term is used to describe software that is easily understood by another programmer?

4. Give one reason why software maintenance is necessary.

Answers 1. User guide and technical guide. **2.** 'Fit for purpose' means that the software does what was agreed at the analysis stage. **3.** Readable. **4.** Errors may be required to be corrected or the client may require new features to be added or the software may be required to operate with new hardware/operating system.

Machine code and high-level languages (HLLs)

Machine code

Machine code is the set of binary code instructions that the computer understands.

```
10010101 10101111
00010001 00111101
11111101 11001101
00001111 00000110
```

Machine code is a very difficult programming language for a human being to program in for several reasons:

1. The instructions and data are represented in binary codes which are difficult to learn.

2. It is easy to make a mistake in entering binary codes which are patterns of 1s and 0s.

3. It is difficult to locate and remove errors.

Top Tip
Some textbooks mention a programming language called 'assembly language', which is halfway between machine code and a high-level language. You do not need to know about assembly language for the purpose of this course.

High-level languages

These are programming languages that use everyday words in the instructions, such as INPUT, IF and REPEAT, that make it much easier to write a program than with machine code. Visual Basic and Java are examples of high-level languages.

```
Let Lenght = Val(Text1.Text)
Let Breadth = Val(Text2.Text)
Let Area = Lenght * Breadth
Picture.Print "The area of the rectangle is"; Area
```

Common features

1. Complex arithmetic can be performed in instructions using +, −, *, /, ^.

2. There are built in functions such as RND, LEFT and ROUND

3. Program instructions can be grouped into subroutines.

4. One HLL instruction translates to several machine code instructions.

5. All HLLs have to be translated into machine code to be run.

Comparison of machine code and high-level languages

It is much harder to write a program in machine code than in a high-level language. However, a program written in machine code will run faster than the equivalent program in an HLL because it is a more efficient process.

Translators

A computer only understands instructions in its own programming language so that high-level languages have to be translated into machine code in order to be run. Interpreters and compilers are two types of translator.

Interpreters

An interpreter translates a high-level language program one instruction at a time when the program is being run. The interpreter is always required to translate and run the program.

Compilers

A compiler translates a high-level language program entirely into machine code before the program is run. A compiler produces a stand-alone machine code program which can run independently of the compiler.

Comparison of interpreters and compilers

1. A compiled program runs faster than an interpreted program, since an interpreted program takes time to translate the instructions at run time.

2. A compiled program uses up less memory than the equivalent interpreted program, since independent machine code is produced with the compiler. The interpreted program always requires the interpreter program and the high-level language to be loaded into main memory at run time.

3. An interpreted program is easier to correct and edit while the program is being developed, since the program can be run again as soon as each change has been made. A compiled program must be re-compiled before it can be run again.

Top Tip
Consider whether the programming language that you use for this course is an interpreted or compiled language. It may be both!

Quick Test

1. What is the name given to a computer's own programming language?
2. Why are some programs still written in machine code even though it is difficult and time-consuming?
3. Does a compiled program or the equivalent interpreted program run faster?
4. Which program translates a high-level language program into machine code before it is run?

Answers 1. Machine code. 2. The program will run faster. 3. The compiled program. 4. Compiler.

Intermediate 2 Computing

Macros and text editors

Macros

A macro is a feature of an application program that allows the user to record a series of actions such as keystrokes and mouse clicks which can then be played back over and over again. The macro can be played back quickly by hitting a keyboard hot key or clicking on a button or graphic.

Macros can also be used to customise a package by writing code to do tasks beyond what is offered by the basic functions of the package.

Many application programs such as Microsoft Word and Excel have a macro facility. The series of actions performed by the user are recorded as a set of program instructions in a scripting language which can then be viewed and edited.

Example

The following macro creates a Word document then formats the font to bold, red and 36 font size. The cursor is then centre-aligned and the text 'KEEP OFF THE GRASS' entered.

```
Sub Macro1()
Documents.Add Template:='Normal', NewTemplate:=False,
DocumentType:=0
Selection.Font.Bold = wdToggle
Selection.Font.Color = wdColorRed
Selection.Font.Size = 36
Selection.ParagraphFormat.Alignment = wdAlignParagraphCenter
Selection.TypeText Text:='KEEP OF THE GRASS'
End Sub
```

KEEP OFF THE GRASS

VBA (Visual Basic for Applications) and JavaScript are commonly used scripting languages.

Examples of the use of macros

The following are typical examples of the use of macros.

1. Putting page numbers with specific formatting into a header/footer.
2. Inserting the user's name, company name, etc. into a document.
3. Automating a mailmerge to produce personalised letters, etc.
4. Changing the page layout of a new document (margins, orientation, paragraph spacing, etc.).

Top Tip
Explore the macro facility in Microsoft Word by using the on-line help, or ask your teacher for help. Record and play back a macro which inserts a footer with your name in italics and centre-aligned.

Advantages of macros

1. Macros can save the user time by quickly playing back a series of actions with one keystroke.
2. Once recorded, macros will always play back accurately.
3. Macros can be used to customise a package.

Text editors

A text editor is a window where the programmer enters the high-level language code.

Features of text editors

Text editors have many features that you would expect to find in a word processing program.

1. Enter and edit text.
2. Copy and paste code.
3. Search and replace text.
4. Automatically indent loops etc.
5. Highlight command words and internal commentary in different colours.

Shown below is a screenshot of a typical text editor.

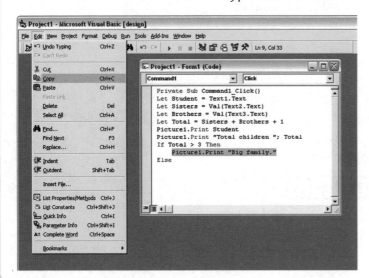

Top Tip

Explore the features of the text editor that you use to create your programs in this course. Investigate how you can change the settings for the automatic formatting of text.

Quick Test

1. How can using a macro save the user time?
2. Give one example of the use of a macro.
3. How can a text editor be used to enter similar instructions efficiently?
4. Name one feature of a text editor.

Answers 1. A series of keystrokes or mouse clicks can be recorded and played back by hitting a hot key or clicking on a button. 2. Any example that customises a package or performs an action that is likely to be repeated. 3. One instruction can be entered and then it can be copied and pasted and edited. 4. Entering text, editing text, automatic formatting of text, etc.

High-level programming language constructs 1

Introduction

Visual Basic is used to illustrate the concepts in the next two topics, since it is the most commonly used language in Scottish schools.

Variables

Programs need to be able to store values which are entered by the user, read in from a backing storage or are the result of a calculation.

A variable is a label given to an item of data so that program instructions can work with them. It is good programming practice to give variables meaningful names such as 'Perimeter' and 'Units' and not 'P' and 'U'.

Data types

There are two data types that you should know for this course.

Numeric: this data type is used to store numbers.

String: this data type is used to store text.

One-dimensional arrays

An array is used to store a list of values of the same data type. Each element of the array is identified by an index number. The example below shows a numeric array called Age(), storing a list of five ages. An index from 0 to 4 is used to identify each element.

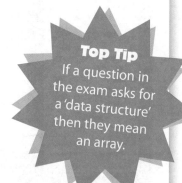

Top Tip
If a question in the exam asks for a 'data structure' then they mean an array.

Age(0)	Age(1)	Age(2)	Age(3)	Age(4)
16	10	13	15	7

Input/output and assignment

Input

The value stored in a variable can be changed as a result of an input command, e.g.:

Let Days = InputBox("Please enter the number of days.")

Output

The value stored in a variable can be displayed, e.g.:

Picture1.Print "Hello Mr" & Surname

Assignment

The value stored in a variable is given a constant value or gets the result
of a calculation, e.g.:

Let Length = 6

Let Volume = 3.14 * Radius ^ 2 * Height

Arithmetic and logical operators

Arithmetic operations

Programming languages perform addition (+), subtraction (–),
multiplication (*) and division (/). The symbol ' ^ ' is used to express
the power of a number. For example, the following instruction calculates
an electricity bill: Let Totalcost = Units * 0.18 + Standingcharge

Logical operations

Programming languages have logical operators (for example, And, Or,
Not) that can be used to implement complex conditions.

1. And

   The following statement is true only if both of the conditions
   Mark > 49 And Mark < 101 are true.

           If Mark > 49 And Mark < 101 Then

2. Or

   The following statement is true if either Percentage < 0 is true
   Or Percentage > 100 is true.

           If Percentage < 0 Or Percentage > 100 Then

3. Not

   The following statement is true if Age < 16 is false.

           If Not (Age < 16) Then

Top Tip

You will not be asked to write a program in the exam but you are expected to know the programming principles shown in this topic.

Quick Test

1. Name two data types found in a programming language.

2. How would the names of 20 pupils be stored in a program?

3. Write an instruction in a language that you know to show how the value 21 is assigned
   to a variable called Age.

4. Write the instruction shown below in a more efficient way.
   Let Volume = Length * Length * Length

Answers 1. Numeric and string. 2. In a one-dimensional array of data type string. 3. Let Age = 21 4. Let Volume = Length ^ 3

High-level programming language constructs 2

Loops

A loop is used in programs to repeat a group of instructions.

Fixed loops

A fixed loop repeats the instructions in the loop a predetermined number of times. The following fixed loop displays the squares of whole numbers from 1–10.

```
For i = 1 To 1
    Picture1.Print i ^ i
Next i
```

Conditional loops

A conditional loop repeats the instructions in the loop as often as necessary until a condition is true. The following conditional loop repeatedly enters a percentage until it is in the range 0 to 100.

```
Do
    Let Percentage = InputBox('Please enter a percentage mark.')
    If Percentage < 0 Or Percentage > 100 Then
    MsgBox ('Not a percentage. Please enter again.')
    End If
Loop Until Percentage >= 0 And Percentage <= 100
```

Top Tip

There are many other versions of loops in programming languages but the examples given in this topic cover the principles of fixed and conditional loops.

Nested loops

A nested loop is a loop that is placed completely inside another loop. The following nested loop uses an outer loop to enter the birthday of 6 celebrities. Within this loop an inner loop repeatedly enters each birthday until it is 6 digits long.

```
For Celebrity = 1 To 6
    Do
        Let Birthday(Celebrity) = InputBox("Please enter a birthday as 6 digits. eg.120687.")
        If Len(Birthday(Celebrity) ) <> 6 Then MsgBox ("Please enter 6 digits.")
    Loop Until Len(Birthday(Celebrity) ) = 6
Next Celebrity
```

Conditional statements

A condition is a statement that is either true or false.

The If ... Else ... End If control construct is used in a program to execute one set of instructions if a condition is true and another set of instructions if a condition is false. The following program branches to one set of instructions if a Mark is greater then 49 and to another set of instructions if a Mark is not greater than 49.

```
If Mark > 49 Then
        Picture1.Print "Pass."
        Let Passes = Passes + 1
Else
        Picture1.Print "Fail."
        Let Fails = Fails + 1
End If
```

Simple conditions

A simple condition depends upon one statement being true or false. The example above uses a simple condition (Mark > 49)

Complex conditions

A complex condition depends upon two or more statements being true or false. Some examples of complex conditions would be:

1. If Mark > 49 And Mark < 60 Then

2. Loop Until Day = 'Mon' Or Day = 'Fri'

Top Tip
An If ... Else ... End If statement is also known as a conditional statement.

Predefined functions

Most programming languages have dozens of predefined functions which can do numeric calculations, manipulate text, format values, etc.

Examples of predefined functions

LEFT ('Macdonald', 3) returns the first 3 characters from the left of the string. i.e. 'Mac'.

ROUND (Depth) rounds the variable Depth to the nearest whole number.

Built-in functions save the programmer time, since there is no need to write the lines of code to do the required calculation.

Quick Test

1. What is a nested loop?

2. What is a conditional loop?

3. Which values for the variable Adolescent make the following complex condition true?
  IF Adolescent > 13 And Adolescent <18 Then

4. What is a predefined function?

Answers 1. A loop that is completely inside another loop. **2.** A conditional loop repeats a set of instructions until a condition is true. **3.** The values 14, 15, 16 and 17 make the complex condition true. **4.** A built-in function that performs a calculation.

Standard algorithms

Introduction

There are algorithms that appear over and over again in computer programs. A programmer may need to find the highest exam mark in a list of marks or the oldest age in a group of students or the longest jump by the competitors in a long-jump competition. Each of these three examples requires an algorithm to find the maximum value in a list of scores. Such an algorithm is called a standard algorithm because the same algorithm is commonly used in different programs.

There are five standard algorithms that you need to know for this course.

Input validation

This algorithm is used to ensure that an entered value is within a valid range. For example, validating that a month entered as a digit is in the range 1 to 12 or that a percentage mark is in the range 0 to 100.

Finding the maximum

This algorithm is used to find the highest value in a list of scores. For example, finding the tallest pupil in a class of children or finding the longest throw for the competitors in a javelin competition.

Finding the minimum

This algorithm is used to find the lowest value in a list of scores. For example, finding the cheapest mobile phone in a mobile phone shop or finding the best time in a 100m race.

Counting occurrences

This algorithm is used to count how many times a given value appears in a list. For example, finding the number of pupils in a class who scored full marks in a test, or finding the number of names in a school roll that begin with 'Mac'.

Linear search

This algorithm is used to find a given value in a list. For example, searching for a specific word in a list of words in a dictionary, or searching for a model of car in a garage stock list.

Top Tip
Don't make the mistake of thinking that the best score in a list is always the maximum value. For example, the best golf score is the minimum value. Sometimes smaller is better.

Pseudocode for input validation

Shown below is pseudocode for the Input validation algorithm.

1. Repeat the following

2.   Get value from user

3.   If value is not within range then

4.   Display an error message

5.   End of if

6. Until value is within range

Top Tip

In this course you are expected to identify which algorithm is required for a given situation. However, you are only expected to understand the details of the Input Validation algorithm and not the other four.

Quick Test

1. What is a standard algorithm?

2. Which standard algorithm would be used to find the best time in a greyhound race?

3. Which standard algorithm would be used to calculate the number of passes in an exam?

4. Which type of loop does an input validation algorithm make use of?

Answers 1. An algorithm such as finding a maximum, counting occurrences, etc. that is commonly found in programs. **2.** Finding the minimum. **3.** Counting occurrences. **4.** A conditional loop.

Test your progress

Questions

1. How many stages are there in the software development process?
2. What is the last stage in the software development process?
3. At which stage of the software development process are structure charts produced?
4. What happens at the implementation stage of the software development process?
5. Give two examples of extreme test data you would choose to validate an exam mark entered as a percentage.
6. Give two items of information that would be included in a technical guide.
7. Give three criteria that can be used to evaluate software.
8. What term is used to describe future modifications to a program to meet changing needs?
9. Which translator translates a high-level language program into machine code while the program is being run?
10. What feature of an application package can be used to customise a package by writing code to do tasks beyond what is offered by the basic functions of the package?
11. How can a text editor automatically make a program more readable?
12. What data structure would a program use to store 7 numbers chosen in a lottery?
13. Is a fixed loop or a conditional loop used in an input validation algorithm?
14. Winston is training to be a programmer for a software development company in New York. Recently he has been given help on the use of predefined functions to speed up the process of writing programs.

    Why do predefined functions speed up the process of software development?
15. A program has been created to process the results of an athletics meeting. Explain why a different algorithm is required for the subroutine that calculates the winner of the hammer throw and the subroutine that calculates the winner of the 400m.
16. At a point in a program a month is entered as a digit and validated in the range 1–12.

    Write pseudocode to show the algorithm for the input validation of the month.

Answers

1. 7
2. Maintenance.
3. Design.
4. The software is written in a suitable language.
5. 0, 100
6. Any two from: Processor requirements; minimum RAM required; hard disc capacity required; operating system platform, etc.
7. Is it fit for purpose, how good is the user interface and readability.
8. Maintenance.
9. Interpreter.
10. A macro.
11. Text editors automatically indent loops, highlight command words in different colours, etc. (see p. 37).
12. An array.
13. A conditional loop.
14. Predefined functions are built-in functions that perform calculations which have been tried and tested. They save programmers time since they do not have to write the lines of code to do the required calculation.
15. Although both algorithms find the best score, the winning score in the hammer throw is the maximum value, whereas the winning score in the 400m is the minimum value.
16. There is more than one way of writing this algorithm but something similar to the following is fine.
    1. Repeat the following
    2.   Get month from user
    3.   If month is not in the range 1–12 then
    4.   Display an error message
    5.   End of if
    6. Until month is in the range 1...12

How did you score

Number of answers correct:

0–6 Not very good. You need to go back and learn this topic.

7–9 Reasonable. You know some of the work but look over before moving on.

10–13 Good. You should move on but go back later and consolidate your knowledge.

14–16 Excellent. You have mastered this topic and can move on.

The development of artificial intelligence 1

Human intelligence

There are many opinions of what is meant by intelligence, however, most people would agree that the following characteristics are aspects of human intelligence.

1. **Communication:** the ability to communicate using language.
2. **Retain Knowledge:** the ability to remember information.
3. **Solve Problems:** the ability to apply known knowledge to adapt to new situations.

Top Tip
AI (Artificial Intelligence) is a computer system that demonstrates behaviour that would be considered to be intelligence if performed by a human.

Turing test

This was a test proposed in 1950 by the mathematician and philosopher Alan Turing to test whether a machine is capable of demonstrating intelligent behaviour. The test involves a person using a computer terminal to communicate with a human and another terminal to communicate with an artificial intelligence system.

The test proposes that if the person cannot tell which terminal is connected to the human and which to the AI system, then the AI system is demonstrating true intelligence.

The Turing test has been criticised because it only tests a limited area of intelligence and does not test areas of intelligence such as imagination and problem-solving. Also, the test depends as much on the intelligence of the person asking the questions as on the intelligence of the human being questioned.

Top Tip
There are plenty of sites on the Internet about Alan Turing and his famous test. Use a search engine to explore the test further.

Representing knowledge

Commonly used languages such as Visual Basic or True Basic do not have the necessary structure and features to allow the creation of AI programs. Programming languages that are used to create AI systems require the storing of facts and rules about a given problem in a knowledge base which can then be used to solve the problem.

Prolog is a programming language that allows the creation of facts and rules in a knowledge base that can then be queried to solve the problem. The following are examples of the sort of facts and rules that could be included in a knowledge base.

Fact or Rule	Meaning
female(Rosie)	Rosie is a female.
male(Alan)	Alan is a male.
eats(sparrow,worms)	A sparrow eats worms.
likes(cat,cream)	A cat likes cream.
mother(X,Y) :- female(X), parent(X,Y)	X is the mother of Y if X is a female and X is parent of Y.

LISP (List Processing) is another programming language used to create AI systems.

Quick Test

1. Give **two** aspects of human intelligence.

2. What is meant by artificial intelligence?

3. Describe the Turing test.

4. Name a programming language used to create programs in artificial intelligence.

Answers 1. Any two from the ability to communicate through language, the retention of knowledge and problem-solving. **2.** A computer system that can perform a task that would be considered to be intelligent if it were performed by a human. **3.** A person communicates with another human and a computer system using computer terminals. If the person cannot tell which then the computer system can be considered to be intelligent. **4.** Prolog or LISP.

The development of artificial intelligence 2

Game-playing programs

Early computer games

The computer games from the 1950s were fairly simple compared to the more complex modern computer games. The early use of AI to play games was restricted to simple games which had a limited set of rules and the progression of play could be easily stored on a computer.

Examples of these early games include noughts and crosses, draughts and chess.

Recent computer games

The improvement of AI programming languages and hardware advances have contributed to a more powerful and widespread use of AI in computer games. These games can learn from previous play where the early games just followed fixed rules.

More recent applications of AI in computer games include Scrabble®, bridge and chess programs that can beat the best human players.

Development of natural language processing (NLP)

Natural language processing is the ability of a computer system to communicate and respond in an intelligent manner to written or spoken words.

Eliza was an early example of an AI program that demonstrated NLP by responding to questions entered by the user in an apparently meaningful way. In reality Eliza merely responded to a limited number of keywords and showed no memory or imagination in its conversation.

A typical conversation with Eliza might go like this:

Eliza: Hello. I am Eliza. How can I help you?

You: I want a puppy for Christmas.

Eliza: Why do you want a puppy for Christmas?

You: So I can take it for walks in the park.

Eliza: Can you elaborate on that?

You: I don't want to elaborate.

Eliza: Why do you not want to elaborate?

Top Tip

Try out Eliza on the Internet by entering 'Eliza' into a search engine.

Chatterbots

These are modern more powerful and complex natural language processing programs which stimulate a more intelligent conversation than the Eliza program. Chatterbots are used to automate telephone answering services that direct calls, airline booking systems, payment of gas bills, etc.

Hardware developments

AI systems can be very complex and require the storage of a huge number of facts and rules in a knowledge base. Also, to query a knowledge base requires a fast processor.

Developments in computer hardware over the past few decades have assisted in the development of AI computer systems by providing the power to allow more and more complex problems to be solved.

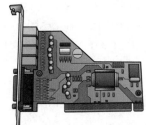

Top Tip
For this course you are expected to know that the key areas of hardware development are faster processors, more main memory and increasing backing storage capacity.

Quick Test

1. Give an example of a computer game that demonstrates the early use of AI from the 1950s.

2. Why are AI systems better at playing games such as draughts rather than Scrabble®?

3. Name a program that performs natural language processing.

4. Give a hardware development that has contributed to the improvement of AI systems.

Answers 1. Noughts and crosses, draughts, chess, etc. **2.** Draughts is more limited in the number of moves that can be made, it is easier to analyse the outcomes of moves, etc. **3.** Eliza or chatterbot. **4.** Any one from faster processors, more main memory and increasing backing storage capacity.

Applications of artificial intelligence 1

Artificial neural systems (ANS)

An artificial neural system is an electronic model of the brain which consists of many simple processors that are interconnected in a network in a way that simulates the connection of nerve cells in the brain.

Artificial neural networks are good in situations where the program's output can be compared to a known output. An ANS can be trained with examples so that it can be used to predict the answer to similar problems once it has learned, by comparing its own output with the known output of the examples.

The uses of ANSs include reading postcodes to help sort mail, making predictions on the stock market, assessing the debt risk of an individual, optical character recognition, etc.

Advantages
An ANS does not require complex logic to solve the problem but simply to adjust the setting of the ANS until its output matches a known output.
An ANS can learn without the need to be reprogrammed.

Disadvantages
The setting up of an ANS is very time-consuming and requires a lot of technical expertise.
An ANS cannot explain the reasoning behind how it made its prediction or decision.

Top Tip

In the exam each question will be worth a certain number of marks. In general make 1 point or give 1 reason for each mark. Use this as a general rule but there is no harm in giving fuller answers if you have time.

Vision systems

Artificial intelligence can be used to recognise or make sense of images. Vision systems require an image to be input into the computer which is then processed to detect edges of objects and make sense of the whole image by relating the identified objects.

There are several difficulties in identifying the objects in an image, such as shadow on objects, objects hiding parts of other objects, etc.

The uses of vision systems include the interpretation of satellite photos for military use and weather forecasting, identifying parts in automated assembly lines, recognising a human face for security reasons, etc.

Top Tip
The objects in an image are identified by matching them with known objects in a database using 'pattern matching'.

Quick Test

1. What is an artificial neural system?

2. Give a use of an ANS in the post office.

3. How does a vision system recognise an object in an image?

4. Give an example of a military use of vision systems.

Answers 1. An electronic model of the brain which consists of interconnected processors that simulate the connection of nerve cells in the brain. **2.** An ANS can be used to automatically sort letters by reading postcodes in order. **3.** The edges of an object are identified and then the object is compared to known objects in a database using pattern matching. **4.** The identification of enemy objects from satellite photos, automated weapons that home in on enemy targets using vision systems, etc.

Applications of artificial intelligence 2

Speech recognition

People speak with different voices and even their own voice can vary from day to day with a sore throat, different moods, etc. Therefore before a speech recognition system can be used it must learn to recognise the voice pattern of the user. This involves the user speaking a selection of words and phrases to train the system.

Top Tip
The morning of the exam, make sure that you have a proper breakfast and arrive at school well before the start of the exam.

Problems

There are several problems that can affect the accuracy of a speech recognition system. Background noise, a sore throat or cold, regional or foreign accents, the use of slang words, etc. can all make it difficult for speech to be accurately recognised.

Uses

Speech recognition can be used as an alternative to keying text into word processing software and mobile phones. These systems have special punctuation commands to tell the difference between text to be entered and punctuation marks such as '.' and ','.

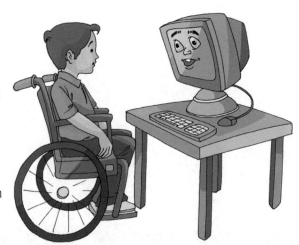

Some modern cars and military vehicles can be controlled by speech recognition which keeps the driver's hands free to control the vehicle. Disabled users who cannot use their hands to enter data can benefit from this technology.

Control instructions

Speech recognition can control machines used in manufacturing by the controller speaking a limited number of control instructions.

Handwriting recognition

This is the conversion of handwritten words into editable text as if it had been typed using a keyboard. Common applications of handwriting recognition are palmtop computers and table PCs where a pen called a stylus is used to write on a touch sensitive screen and handwriting recognition software converts it into editable text.

Top Tip
There is a similarity between speech and handwriting recognition in that both systems need training to learn the particular speech and writing of a user.

Training

Since there is a lot of variation in people's handwriting it is sometimes necessary to train the system to be able to recognise the particular shapes of characters written by a particular user.

Quick Test

1. What must be done before a speech recognition system can operate effectively?

2. Give **two** problems associated with a speech recognition system.

3. Name a hardware device that uses handwriting recognition.

4. Suggest a group of users which may not benefit from a computer system that uses handwriting recognition?

Answers 1. The system must be trained to recognise the user's speech pattern. **2.** Any two from background noise, sore throat, foreign accent, etc. **3.** A palmtop computer, table PC, etc. **4.** Certain disabled users.

Applications of artificial intelligence 3

Intelligent robots

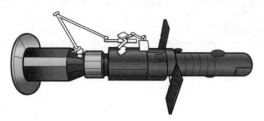

An intelligent robot is able to adjust what it does according to the conditions and not just blindly carry out a set task. It uses sensors to detect what is happening in its environment and takes an action based upon what is happening.

Top Tip
Commonly used sensors are bump, infra red, touch, magnetic, light, heat, sound, humidity, smoke and pressure sensors.

Applications of intelligent robots

1. The automated delivery of goods in warehouses.

2. The inspection of pipes on the seabed or underground.

3. They are used in bomb disposal.

4. The exploration of unknown environments such as the ocean floor.

Advantages of intelligent robots

1. Intelligent robots are often used in situations where it would be dangerous for humans, such as in space.

2. They are more accurate than humans at carrying out tasks.

3. Robots do not get wages but there is a high initial cost of installing the robots.

4. They can work 24/7 without getting tired.

Expert systems

An expert system is a program that mimics the advice of an expert based upon information provided by human experts. They are used in areas such as medicine, law, financial planning, machine repair, etc. to make a diagnosis and give advice.

An expert system has three components:

1. A knowledge base which contains a set of facts and rules about the problem.

2. An explanatory interface which asks questions to get input from the user.

3. An inference engine, which draws a conclusion or makes a diagnosis based upon the facts and rules.

The expert system can also provide an explanation of how it arrived at the conclusion.

Advantages of expert systems

1. The expertise is always available and there is no delay in acquiring an expert.

2. After the initial cost of buying the system there is no charge for a human expert's advice, which can be expensive.

3. It combines the expertise of several experts, and therefore contains more knowledge than one human could have.

4. There is less chance of error since the system will not make a careless mistake.

Issues

Many people are concerned that a machine is making very important decisions which are a matter of life and death. There is also the legal issue of who is to blame when something goes wrong as the result of the advice given by an expert system. Most expert systems come with a disclaimer stating that it is the user who is responsible for the consequences of its use. Social issues include the loss of jobs and the reduction of human expertise. Expert systems can also require considerable training for the users.

Top Tip

In the exam, make sure that you show the working in any questions that require calculations. Even if your final answer is wrong you will probably pick up some of the marks.

Quick Test

1. What items of hardware does an intelligent robot have that allows it to adapt to what is happening in its enviroment?

2. Give a hazardous environment where intelligent robots could be used instead of humans.

3. What type of computer software would be useful in a school for guidance staff to use to suggest suitable careers to students based on their interests?

4. Give an area of application of an expert system.

Answers 1. Sensors. 2. In space, the seabed, areas of radiation, bomb disposal, etc. 3. An expert system. 4. Medicine, law, machine repair, etc.

Search techniques

Problem-solving by search

The solution to a problem in artificial intelligence can be represented by a series of choices. For example, in a game the first move can be a choice of several moves, each of these moves then leads to a choice of second move and so on. In a complex AI problem the number of possible moves can quickly grow to millions and millions of combinations when looking as little as ten moves ahead.

Top Tip

Hardware improvements such as faster processors and larger memory capacities have contributed to better AI systems since it has allowed the processing and storing of much more complex search trees.

The series of steps can be represented in a diagram called a search tree.

Breadth first and depth first searches

AI programs use a problem solving technique which examines all solutions until a match if found.

Breadth first and depth first are two search techniques each of which has its own rules to determine the order in which the elements of the search tree are visited.

The search tree shown can be used to illustrate how a breadth first and a depth first operates.

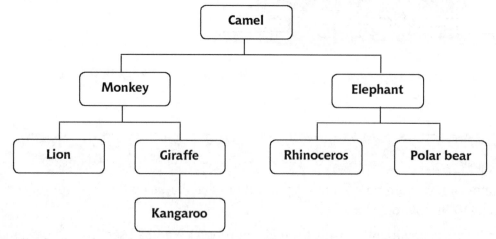

Breadth first

In this search technique each horizontal layer (starting with the top layer) of the search tree is searched from left to right in turn. The order of visiting the elements of the search tree is:

Camel, Monkey, Elephant, Lion, Giraffe, Rhinoceros, Polar bear, Kangaroo.

Depth first

This search technique starts with the left-hand side of the search tree and searches down a branch until a solution is found. If a solution is not found by the end of the branch then the search backtracks to the last place where there was a choice of paths, and a search is made down the next branch and so on. The order of visiting the elements of the search tree is:

Camel, Monkey, Lion, Giraffe, Kangaroo, Elephant, Rhinoceros, Polar bear.

Top Tip
There has always been a question on breadth first and depth first searches in the Intermediate 2 exam, so make sure you know how they work.

Quick Test

1. Which search technique starts by searching the top horizontal layer for a solution?

2. Which search technique starts by searching down the first branch on the left of the search tree?

3. A problem is presented using the search tree shown.

   The solution to the problem is Harry.

   What is the order of visiting the elements of the tree for a breadth first search to reach the solution?

4. What would the order of visiting the elements of the tree be if a depth first search was used?

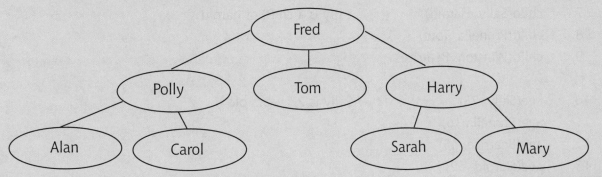

Knowledge representations

Semantic net

Artificial intelligence programs cannot solve a problem without storing information about the problem in a knowledge base. A semantic net is a diagram that is used to represent known facts about a problem by displaying a group of objects and the relationships between them.

For example, a semantic net can be used to represent the following facts:

is_a(mango,fruit)   eats(monkey,fruit)
is_a(banana,fruit)   eats (monkey,nuts)

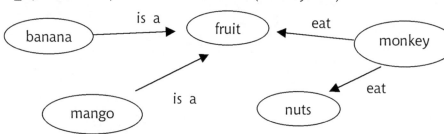

Top Tip
In the exam you may be asked to create a simple semantic net given a list of objects and some relationships between them.

Facts, rules and queries

The programming language Prolog is used in this topic to define the facts and rules in a knowledge base that can then be queried to solve the problem.

A knowledge base describing information about some people in a family is shown below.

1.	male(Harold)	Harold is a male
2.	male(Winston)	
3.	male(Tom)	
4.	female(Sally)	Sally is a female
5.	female(Prunella)	
6.	female(Beatrice)	
7.	child(Sally, Harold)	Sally is a child of harold
8.	child(Prunella, Tom)	
9.	child(Winston, Beatrice)	
10.	age(Sally, 23)	Sally is 23 years old
11.	age(Prunella,16)	
12.	age(Beatrice, 45)	
13.	age(Harold, 52)	
14.	age(Tom, 39)	

15.   age(Winston,12)

16.   daughter(X,Y) if female(X)   X is a daughter of Y if X is a
      and child(X,Y)   female and X is a child of Y

17.   boy(X) if male(X) and   X is a boy if X is a male and the
      age(X,Y) and Y<18   age of X is Y and Y is less than 18

The knowledge base can then be interrogated with queries. The following examples cover the kind of queries that are regularly asked for in the Intermediate 2 exam.

Example 1
The result of the query ?male(Tom) is true since a match is made at line 3.

Example 2
The result of the query ?child(Sally,Tom) is false since a match fails.

Example 3
The first solution of the query ?daughter(X,Tom) can be shown in a manual trace as follows:

The solution requires the matching of the two subgoals female(X) and child(X,Tom).

The first sub goal female(X) matches at line 4 X=Sally.

The second subgoal child(Sally,Tom) fails X=Sally is not a solution.

Backtrack to line 5.

The first subgoal female(X) matches at line 5 X=Prunella.

The second subgoal child(Prunella,Tom) matches at line 8.

X=Prunella is the solution.

Example 4
The first solution of the query ?boy(X) can be shown in a manual trace as follows:

The first subgoal male(X) matches at line 1 X=Harold.

The second subgoal age(X,Y) fails at line 13 since Y is not less than 18.

Backtrack to line 2.

The first subgoal male(X) matches at line 2 X=Winston.

The second subgoal age(X,Y) matches at line 15 since Y<18.

X=Winston is the solution.

Top Tip
Look through past exam papers for this type of question and their solutions. They are fairly repetitive so it should give you a feel for what you can expect to be asked in your own exam.

Quick Test

1. Which diagram can be used to display a group of objects and the relationships between them?

2. How many subgoals are there in the query ?daughter(X)?

3. What is the result of the query ?child(Sally,Beatrice)?

4. What is the result of the query ?daughter(X,Harold)?

Answers 1. A semantic net. 2. Two. 3. False. 4. sally.

Test your progress

Questions

1. Give an aspect of human intelligence that is not demonstrated by modern artificial intelligence systems.
2. What is meant by the term 'artificial intelligence'?
3. Give a flaw of the Turing test.
4. What hardware developments have contributed to the increasing success of AI in playing games?
5. What is contained in an expert system knowledge base?
6. What is a chatterbot?
7. Give an example of the use of an artificial neural system in banking.
8. A vision recognition system is used to identify enemy tanks in a battlefield. Suggest a problem that could affect the accuracy of this system.
9. What legal issues might result from using an expert system in medicine?
10. Draw a semantic net to illustrate the following facts.

   is_a(Wendy, Girl)   is_a(Paul, Boy)

   likes (Wendy, Tennis)   likes(Paul, Golf)   likes(Paul, Tennis)

11. A railway station uses a speech recognition system in automated machines where passengers can buy tickets. Suggest a possible problem that could prevent this system from working properly.
12. How can a company that creates expert systems protect itself in case the advice given by its systems leads to disastrous consequences?
13. What are the advantages of using robots in car assembly plants?
14. A home for the future is equipped with an artificial intelligence system that responds to spoken commands such as CLOSE CURTAINS, TV ON, HEATING HIGH, etc.
    What area of AI is being used to understand the commands?
15. A problem is represented by the search tree shown below.
    List the order of visiting the nodes in a:

    (a) breadth first search   **(b)** depth first search.

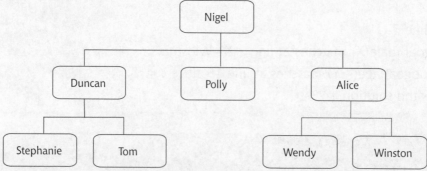

16. A knowledge base holds some facts and rules about some actors.

    1. singer(Alice, good)   6. age(Polly, 16)
    2. singer(Polly, excellent)   7. age(Fred, 20)
    3. singer(Fred, excellent)   8. age(Gary, 17)
    4. singer(Gary, fair)   9. gets_audition(X) if singer(X, excellent)
    5. age(Alice, 19)   and age(X, Y) and Y>17

Using the numbering system above trace the following query as far as the first solution.?gets_audition(X)

Answers

1. Imagination, creativity, etc.
2. A computer system that demonstrates behaviour that would be considered intelligent if it were performed by a human.
3. The Turing test tests a restricted area of intelligence and depends on the intelligence of the human interrogator and the human being interrogated.
4. Increased processor speeds, higher capacity main memory and backing storage devices, etc.
5. Rules and facts about the problem.
6. A natural language processing program which simulates an intelligent conversation.
7. Debt risk assessment, stock market predictions, etc.
8. There could be shadows on the tanks, tanks hiding parts of other tanks, etc.
9. Who is legally responsible if things go wrong.
10.

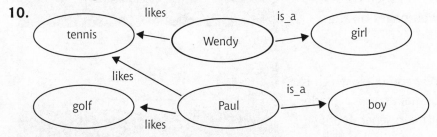

11. Background noise.
12. Include a disclaimer.
13. Robots can work 24/7, do not go on strike, produce more, etc.
14 Speech/voice recognition.
15. **(a)** Nigel, Duncan, Polly, Alice, Stephanie, Tom, Wendy, Winston.
    (b) Nigel, Duncan, Stephanie, Tom, Polly, Alice, Wendy, Winston
16. The first subgoal singer(X,excellent) matches at line 2 X=Polly.
    The second subgoal age(Polly,Y) fails at line 6 since Y>17 is false.
    Backtrack to line 3.
    The subgoal singer(X,excellent) matches at line 3 X=Fred
    The second subgoal age(Fred,Y) matches at line 7 since Y >17 is true.
    X=Fred

How did you score

Number of answers correct:

0–6 Not very good. You need to go back and learn this topic.

7–9 Reasonable. You know some of the work but look over before moving on.

10–13 Good. You should move on but go back later and consolidate your knowledge.

14–16 Excellent. You have mastered this topic and can move on.

Network applications 1

The Internet

The Internet provides various services including access to the World Wide Web (WWW), the transference of files and email.

World Wide Web (WWW)

The World Wide Web is a vast amount of multimedia data (text, graphics, video and sound) stored in the form of web pages.

URL (Universal Resource Locator)

Each web page is identified by a unique address called a URL (Universal Resource Locator).

1. Protocol

A protocol is a set of rules required for successful transmission. HTTP (Hypertext Transfer Protocol) is the protocol used for the successful transmission of web pages on the Internet.

2. Domain name

This is the address of the server computer which is hosting the web page. The domain name is made up of two or more parts which are separated by dots.

The parts are used to specify the type of organisation and the country where the site is based.

Part	Meaning
.com	A company
.edu	Educational institution
.gov	Governmental agency
.org	Non-profit-making organisation

Part	Country
.uk	United Kingdom
.fr	France
.au	Australia

3. Path

This specifies the pathway or route to the file.

4. File

This is the name of the file being accessed. in this case: help.htm.

Top Tip
Some books will expand URL as **Uniform** Resource Locator but for the purpose of this course make sure that you use **Universal** Resource Locator. The structure of a URL is illustrated here.

FTP (File Transfer Protocol)

Files are downloaded and uploaded on the Internet using the FTP protocol. The example shows a URL for a file transfer site used to download extra features to games programs.

ftp:// www.bestpatches.com

Protocol   Server name

Top Tip
Netiquette is a term used to describe good and bad behaviour when sending emails. Enter the word 'netiquette' into a search engine to find out more about codes of conduct applied to sending emails

Electronic mail (email)

The structure of an email address and the facilities provided in email programs has already been dealt with in Unit 2: Computer Systems.

However the Computer Networking unit in the exam has asked for knowledge of a code of conduct when sending emails so it will be covered here.

Code of conduct

1. Always put a word or phrase in the subject line of the email.

2. Do not write in block capitals; this is called shouting as it looks aggressive.

3. Do not send an email that is intended to incite anger; this is called flaming.

Web browser

A browser is a program that displays web pages and allows the user to navigate around web pages and websites. Commonly used browsers include Internet Explorer and Netscape navigator.

In addition to displaying web pages and navigating the Internet, browsers have the following features:

1. Keeping a history of visited websites.

2. Keeping a list of favourite websites.

3. Sending and receiving of emails.

4. Performing file transfer.

5. Customising settings for the browser.

Quick Test

1. Sam enters http://www.oldjokes.co.uk into a browser. Which Internet service is Sam using?

2. Name the four parts of a URL.

3. What does FTP stand for?

4. What is the purpose of a browser?

Answers **1.** The World Wide Web. **2.** Protocol, domain name, pathway, file. **3.** File Transfer Protocol. **4.** A browser is a program that displays web pages and allows the user to navigate around web pages and websites.

Network applications 2

See also Unit 2: Networking 2, p. 20.

Browsers and microbrowsers

A microbrowser is a small-scale browser that is used in handheld devices such as mobile phones and PDAs. A microbrowser operates with less memory, a smaller screen and a slower connection than a browser so it provides fewer features such as multimedia functions and text formatting than a full-scale browser.

The WAP (Wireless Application Protocol) is used by a microbrowser to transfer Internet content.

A browser uses the HTTP protocol but a microbrowser uses the WAP protocol.

Top Tip
Remember the different protocols used by browsers and microbrowsers to transfer web pages.

Web pages

A web page can be considered as a multimedia document with hyperlinks to other web pages.

In the past, web pages were created with a programming language called HTML, but nowadays they can be created much more quickly using programs such as Dreamweaver and FrontPage.

Navigation

Browsers provide several means of navigating between web pages.

1. A URL can be entered into the browser.

2. Backward and forward arrows allow the user to quickly view previously visited sites and then return forward.

3. Saving favourites can provide a quick link to frequently visited sites.

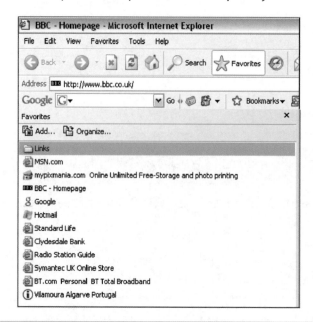

ISP (Internet Service Provider)

The purpose of an ISP is to provide access to computers connected to the Internet. Examples of commonly used ISPs are AOL, Pipex and BT.

In addition to providing a connection to the Internet, an ISP will normally provide the following services:

1. A filtering service to block inappropriate web pages.

2. Anti-virus software.

3. An email address.

4. An area of web space to which the user can upload their own web pages.

Quick Test

1. What is the difference between a browser and a microbrowser?

2. How can a hyperlink be found on a web page?

3. How can Japanese flower-arranging sites be found on the Internet if the user does not know any particular sites?

4. What is the function of an ISP?

Answers 1. A microbrowser is a small-scale browser that is used in handheld devices such as mobile phones to surf the Internet, but is more limited and has fewer features than a browser which is used on a desktop or laptop computer. **2.** A hyperlink is usually found by looking for a piece of coloured text or an image to click on. **3.** The user can enter relevant keywords and phrases into a search engine. **4.** An ISP provides access to computers on the Internet.

E-commerce and converging technologies

E-commerce

E-commerce is the use of the Internet to conduct business and provide services.
Companies use the Internet for e-marketing and e-sales of their products.

Advantages	
1.	The entire world becomes the market place since anyone who has Internet access becomes a potential customer.
2.	There is less need for the expense of shops, staff, etc.
3.	People can shop 24 hours a day and 7 days a week.
4.	Goods can be bought from home without the time spent and cost of travelling.
5.	The price of goods and services bought on-line is usually cheaper.
Disadvantages	
1.	There is the possibility of credit card fraud although more secure payment methods are being developed.
2.	There can be a high cost of setting up and maintaining the website.
3.	Goods may not be as good a quality as expected when actually seen and touched.
4.	The goods can take several weeks to arrive.
5.	Customers who do not have the technology cannot be contacted.

E-government
The government is increasingly using the Internet to keep people informed about policies and to provide services such as the paying of road tax and community charge, etc.

Top Tip
Talk to someone who has bought goods by e-commerce and ask them about the advantages and disadvantages of this method of shopping.

Converging technologies

The term 'converging technologies' refers to home appliances with built-in internal and external communication capability. These devices provide several multimedia technology functions in a single device.

A mobile phone is an example of converging technologies. It provides the functions of a phone, Internet access, email, games, etc. Other examples of converging technologies are digital TV, games consoles, PDAs (Personal Digital Assistants) etc. (See also Unit 6: Synthesised sound and implications of multimedia technology, p. 90.)

Top Tip

Prepare for the prelim exam by using this book. Your performance in the prelim can be used by your school for an appeal, so get the best mark possible and do not leave things to the final exam.

Quick Test

1. Wendy works during the day and has no time to go to the shops. How can e-commerce be of use to Wendy?

2. Give a reason why e-commerce cannot be considered to be a global service at present.

3. Give an example of a converging technology device.

4. What is meant by the term 'converging technologies'?

Answers 1. With E-commerce Wendy can shop 24 hours a day so she can buy goods in the evening or at night. **2.** E-commerce is only available to people who have Internet access. Very few people in places such as poor African countries have Internet access. **3.** Mobile phone, PDA, digital television, etc. **4.** A single device with a built-in internal and external communication capability that provides several multimedia technology functions.

Implications of networks

Economic implications of networks

The growth of network technologies and the Internet has consequences for business and education.

Consequences for business

1. Large businesses can easily share information and communicate between offices.
2. Communication by email with customers anywhere in the world.
3. The cost of networks and keeping them secure can be high.

Consequences for education

1. Schools and colleges have improved administration and communications systems due to computer networks.
2. Networks and the Internet provide a virtually limitless supply of information to help students in research and learning.
3. Installing and maintaining a network in a school can take up a considerable percentage of the school budget.

Regulation of Investigatory Powers Act 2000

Since the computer networks and the Internet became prevalent in the workplace as a tool in business and education, employers have become concerned that their employees are wasting time using these facilities to play games, send personal emails, etc.

The Regulation of Investigatory Powers Act 2000 is a law that gives employers the right to monitor the activities of their employees to make sure that what they are doing is work-related.

An argument for the act

Some people believe that employers should have the right to monitor their employees to make sure the employee is not carrying out their own personal business at the company's expense and in company time.

An argument against the act

Some people believe that employees should have the right to privacy when sending emails, making telephone calls, etc. and that the Act is against the freedom of speech.

Top Tip

Research the Regulation of Investigatory Powers Act 2000 on the Internet and gain a deeper knowledge of this Act.

Code of Conduct

There is a need for employees and children to adhere to a code of conduct in the workplace and in schools in the use of networks and the Internet. These organisations often insist that the network users sign a form called 'an acceptable use policy' that states what will and will not be tolerated.

The code of conduct will contain rules such as:

1. Do not download offensive materials.
2. Do not use offensive language.
3. Do not distribute harmful materials such as viruses.

Top Tip
Find out if your school has a code of conduct for the staff and/ or students and what it specifies about the use of the network and the Internet.

Quick Test

1. Give two advantages to an international company of using a computer network.
2. What is the advantage of providing Internet access in schools?
3. What is the name of the act that allows employers to monitor the work done by their employees?
4. What can schools do to make the students adhere to a code of conduct when using the school network and the Internet?

Answers 1. They can share data between offices globally and there is quick and easy communication using email. 2. Students can use the Internet as a tool for research and learning. 3. The Regulation of Investigatory Powers Act 2000. 4. The school can insist that the students sign an acceptable use policy.

Network security

Security measures

Security of data means that data stored on a computer is private and safe. Computer networks require protection against unauthorised access and attacks.

The security can be implemented through physical or software measures.

Physical

This uses actual physical security such as locks on doors, locks on keyboards, etc.

Software

Access to networks is usually controlled by the user logging on with a user ID and password. Each user is given access rights by the network operating system to restrict what the user can do. Different users are given different levels of access rights to restrict them to the services they require to do their work and no more.

NEVER SHARE YOUR PASSWORD

Top Tip
Ask the network manager at your school what security exists on your school network to add depth to your understanding of this topic.

Encryption

Encryption is a method of security where confidential data is encoded so that even if it is hacked into, the data is not of any use to the hackers. The data is decoded by a software key to turn it back into its original state.

ENCRYPTION

Filtering Internet content

There are many websites that contain unsuitable material for children. Many organisations such as schools and businesses use filtering software to block access to offensive sites.

Top Tip
You could talk about walled gardens and firewalls as examples of software that filters web pages to add depth to your answers.

Potential threats

The following are different types of threat to network security:

Hardware failure

There are many hardware components on a network that can fail and bring down part or all of a network. These include the computers, servers, printers, transmission cables, routers, etc.

Software failure

Often software can fail due to bugs in the code, the network operating system can become corrupted, etc.

Data transmission failure

Transmission cables can be broken or damaged or the data can become corrupted due to interference from electrical and magnetic sources.

Physical disasters

All networks are subject to physical damage from disasters such as fire, flooding, terrorist attacks, etc.

Backup strategy

Loss of data to a large organisation such as a bank or a dental practice would be catastrophic. It is essential that these organisations keep backup copies of their data so that they can recover up-to-date data in case of loss or damage. It is important that backups are performed regularly and that they are kept in a secure location.

High-capacity backing storage media such as magnetic tape, DVD etc. are used for these backups.

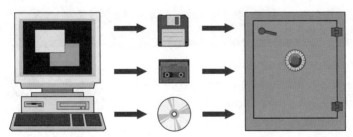

Quick Test

1. How does a user on a computer network log on to his/her account?

2. What is encryption?

3. How can a family protect their children from viewing unsuitable material on the Internet?

4. Why is it that organisations can often recover quickly from loss of data from a virus attack?

Answers 1. A user logs on by entering a user ID and a password. 2. Encryption is the encoding of data so that it is meaningless if it is accessed by a hacker. 3. The family can use filtering software that will block access to unsuitable sites. 4. If they have a backup copy of up-to-date data then they can recover the data from the backup.

Data transmission

Types of transmission

Unicast
This term describes a type of transmission where data is transmitted from one sender to one receiver.

Broadcast
This term describes a type of transmission where data is transmitted to all of the computers on a network.

Multicast
This term describes a type of transmission where one sender transmits to a group of receivers at the same time. An example of multicast is where one email message is sent to several people in an address book at the same time.

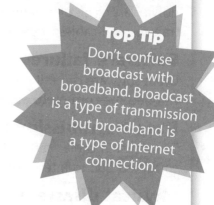

Top Tip
Don't confuse broadcast with broadband. Broadcast is a type of transmission but broadband is a type of Internet connection.

Voice and data transmission

Traditionally computer networks were used to transmit data, however there is an increasing use of computer networks for voice transmissions to allow people to speak to each other.

Additional hardware and software is necessary for voice and data transmission, which includes microphones, speakers and voice communications software.

Wireless networks

Wireless connections provide freedom of movement, and the absence of cabling makes for a less cluttered and safer working environment. Wireless connections are slower than cable connections but the technology is improving all the time and is becoming popular in offices as well as homes.

WPAN (wireless personal area network)
A WPAN uses wireless transmissions to connect various devices used by an individual person. Typically it is used to connect devices such as laptops, PDAs, printers and mobile phones. Bluetooth is a slow-speed wireless connection used over short distances for this type of wireless network.

Wireless LAN
This is a LAN where conventional cables have been replaced with wireless connections. A wireless LAN has a slower transmission speed than a conventional LAN and is less secure, but has the advantage that laptop computers can easily be moved around as required.

Additional hardware required for a wireless LAN

A computer is connected to a wireless LAN using a wireless NIC (Network Interface Card). The network also requires a receiver and a transmitter to accept and send data

Wireless WAN

This is a WAN where the conventional links of telecommunications connections have been replaced with wireless connections. There are various wireless links in use, including wireless receivers and transmitters mounted on buildings, satellite links, mobile phone connections, etc.

Increasing in popularity is mobile broadband, which provides Internet access through a small portable modem plugged into a laptop. This allows a laptop to access the Internet from a variety of locations, but is still fairly expensive.

Top Tip
Avoid giving very brief answers when asked to give an advantage or disadvantage in the exam. Give full answers that provide a reason or explanation for the advantage or disadvantage.

Quick Test

1. What is meant by the term unicast?

2. Which type of data transmission is being used when an email is being sent to a group of people in a mailing list at the same time?

3. What extra hardware is required for a WLAN compared to a LAN?

4. What does WPAN stand for?

Answers 1. Unicast is where data is transmitted from one sender to one receiver. 2. Multicast. 3. A receiver, transmitter and wireless NIC. 4. Wireless Personal Area Network.

Internet connections

Types of connection

There are many different types of Internet connection available. When choosing a suitable type of connection for a given situation the bandwidth (speed of data transmission) and cost are important.

Dial-up modem
Dial-up is a slow Internet connection which requires a connection to be made to the ISP at the start of a session, which can cause a wait of a few minutes.

Cable modem
Cable modem is a very fast Internet connection that uses the cable television network for transmission, with a speed many times faster than a dial-up connection. The connection is always on and there is no waiting time to connect. However, cable modem has the disadvantage of being a more expensive connection than dial-up.

The high bandwidth of a cable modem connection makes it suitable for watching live videos and downloading music.

Leased line
Large companies lease connections from a telecommunications company. This means that they have the sole use of a high speed, dedicated line which is always on. This type of connection is very expensive.

ISDN (Integrated Services Digital Network)
This is a dial-up connection that uses digital transmission which has been largely superseded by faster connection methods.

ADSL (Asymmetric Digital Subscriber Line)
This connection provides a high speed, always-on connection for homes and businesses that uses ordinary telephone lines. It permits data and voice transmissions to be carried out at the same time.

Broadband
The term 'broadband' is used to describe a very fast Internet connection. A cable modem connection commonly used by home users is often described as a broadband connection.

Top Tip

A common exam question asks you to choose a suitable Internet connection to meet the requirements of a given situation, and to justify your answer. Remember that transmitting video and sound data requires a broadband connection because of its fast bandwidth.

Domain name service (DNS)

Domain names

Organisations are identified on the Internet by a domain name such as Microsoft.com or BBC.co.uk. Domain names are used because they are easy for people to remember, but the Internet uses an IP address to identify and retrieve web pages.

Top Tip
In the exam you do not need to answer the questions in the order 1, 2, 3 ... You may wish to start with questions that you know well to help you gain confidence before taking on topics you find more difficult.

The domain name service (DNS) takes the domain name and changes it into its associated IP address. This DNS works by looking up a database which keeps a list of domain names together with their IP address.

Host name resolution

This is the name given to the process of changing a domain name into its associated IP address.

Quick Test

1. Give one advantage of a cable modem connection over a dial-up connection.

2. Why would a company use expensive leased lines for their Internet connection?

3. What is meant by the term 'broadband'?

4. What is the function of the DNS?

Answers 1. Any one from faster bandwidth, always connected, you can use the Internet and the phone at the same time, etc. **2.** The company can have the sole use of a high speed, dedicated line which is always on. **3.** A very fast Internet connection. **4.** The DNS (Domain Name Service) takes the domain name entered by the user and searches a database to find the associated IP address.

Test your progress

Questions

1. What does URL stand for?

2. Wendy enters ftp://www.rock.com into a browser. Which Internet service is Wendy using?

3. What does it mean if a domain name ends in .org.uk?

4. What is the name of the software that is used to display Internet content on a mobile phone?

5. What is a hyperlink in a web page?

6. Apart from providing a connection to computers on the Internet, give another facility usually provided by an ISP.

7. Give an example of e-government.

8. What term is used to describe a home appliance with a built-in communications capability?

9. What are the financial implications to the customer of e-commerce?

10. Give an argument against the Regulation of Investigatory Powers Act 2000.

11. What are the requirements of a good backup strategy?

12. What is meant by the type of data transmission called broadcast?

13. What is the name of the wireless connection used on a WPAN?

14. Polly works as a network manager in a university. She is currently leading a project to replace a conventional LAN in the science block with a wireless LAN.

    What are the advantages and disadvantages of this change?

15. Marco spends a lot of time on the Internet watching live video of cricket test matches and downloading rock music.

    Which type of Internet connection is suitable for someone who is regularly watching live video and downloading music from Internet sites?

16. Stephanie likes to play chess and every Sunday evening she accesses the web page www.chessworld.com to play against other chess players from around the world.

    Once Stephanie has entered the URL the domain name service carries out domain name resolution to retrieve the web page.

    Explain what happens during domain name resolution.

Answers

1. Universal Resource Locator.
2. Wendy is using the file transfer service.
3. It means that it is the website of a non-profit-making organisation in the United Kingdom.
4. Microbrowser.
5. It is a link to another web page or website usually activated by clicking on a piece of coloured text or an image.
6. Any one from: filtering offensive web pages; anti-virus software; providing an area of web space; email account etc.
7. Any one from: up-to-date information about laws and local government; on-line opinion polls; voting in elections, etc.
8. Converging technologies device.
9. Money is saved in travelling costs and usually the goods are cheaper to buy.
10. Employees should have a right to privacy and the Act is against the principles of freedom of speech.
11. A good backup strategy requires making regular up-to-date backups and keeping backups in a secure place.
12. Data is transmitted to all of the computers on a network.
13. Bluetooth.
14. A wireless LAN has a slower transmission speed than a conventional LAN and is less secure, but has the advantage that laptop computers can easily be moved around as required.
15. A broadband connection, because it has a fast bandwidth that is required for transmitting high capacity multimedia data such as video and sound.
16. The domain name service looks up the URL entered by Stephanie in a database and finds the associated IP address.

How did you score

Number of answers correct:

0–6 Not very good. You need to go back and learn this topic.

7–9 Reasonable. You know some of the work but look over before moving on.

10–13 Good. You should move on but go back later and consolidate your knowledge.

14–16 Excellent. You have mastered this topic and can move on.

The development process

The development process for a multimedia application

The process of developing a multimedia application follows the same seven stages you met earlier in the Software Development unit. The stages are analysis, design, implementation, testing, documentation, evaluation and maintenance.

Analysis
The requirements of the client for the multimedia application are identified and a complete and detailed description of the project is drawn up.

Design
The screen layouts for the multimedia application are determined. Storyboarding is a technique that is used to describe the layout of the multimedia elements of each screen, to specify the links between the screens, etc.

Implementation
The design of the multimedia application is turned into a working application, usually with an authoring package.

Testing
Tests take place to make sure that sound and video files play properly, links between screens operate correctly, etc.

Documentation
A user guide is produced to help the clients to use the features of the multimedia application and a technical guide is produced to support technical staff in its installation and maintenance.

Evaluation
The multimedia application is evaluated against a set of criteria to ensure that it meets the requirements of the client.

Maintenance
In the future modifications may need to be made to the multimedia application, for instance: to remove previously undetected errors; to adapt to changes in the hardware or software environment; or to add new features requested by the user.

Top Tip
Multimedia applications are programs that contain text, graphics, video and sound data.

Top Tip
Make sure that you have the right equipment for the exam. Two or more pens and pencils, a ruler and a working calculator are essential.

Creation of multimedia applications

Authoring packages

Multimedia authoring software is a program that allows the application to be created by dragging and dropping the multimedia elements onto the page.

A stand-alone executable file is created which can be run by itself without the need for the software that was used to create it.

Presentation software

Presentation packages allow the creation of a multimedia slide show with links between the slides.

The presentation file requires a file player program to display the slide show.

Creation of websites

Text editors

Web pages can be created by entering HTML (Hypertext Markup Language) code into a text editor.

This requires a lot of technical expertise and is very time-consuming.

WYSIWYG (What You See Is What You Get) editors

A WYSIWYG editor allows web pages to be created without the need for a knowledge of HTML code simply by dragging and dropping the web page elements such as titles, hyperlinks, tables, etc. onto the page.

WYSIWYG editors let the creator see exactly what the web page will look like as it is created and include a preview feature.

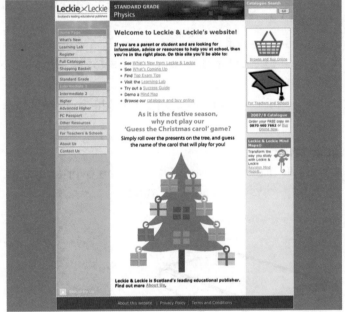

Web browsers

A web browser is a program needed to display web pages and to allow the user to navigate between them.

Quick Test

1. At which stage of the development of a multimedia project is a storyboard produced?

2. What takes place at the testing stage in the development of a multimedia application?

3. What does WYSIWYG stand for?

4. Name the application software that is used to display web pages.

Answers 1. Design. 2. Tests are made to ensure that sound and video files play properly, links between screens operate correctly, etc. 3. What You See Is What You Get. 4. A browser.

Bit-mapped graphics data 1

Hardware used to capture bit-mapped graphics

Several hardware devices can be used to capture bit-mapped graphics images. The most commonly used devices are digital cameras and scanners.

Digital camera

A digital camera uses an array of CCDs (Charge-Coupled Devices) to capture the light emitted by an image and turn it into a voltage that can then be entered into a computer. Each CCD captures the data for one pixel.

The images can be stored on a memory card that typically has a capacity of around 4 Gb.

The advantages of storing images on a memory card are that unwanted images can be deleted, and it can be easily removed to insert into a printer or a computer.

Unlike traditional photographic film, the memory card can be used over and over again.

Scanner

A scanner uses a line of CCDs that scan over an image on paper capturing rows of pixels as it moves.

Top Tip

Learn this topic then get a friend or a member of your family to ask you questions about it.

Storage of graphics data

Bit-mapped graphics files take up a lot of storage so compression techniques have been developed to reduce the file size. The compression is either 'lossless' or 'lossy'.

Lossless compression reduces the file size without any loss of detail or quality.

Lossy compression reduces the file size at the expense of detail and quality.

File formats

1. Bitmap

   This is an uncompressed file format where a binary code is stored for the colour of each pixel.

2. GIF (Graphics Interchange Format)

This is a file format that uses lossless compression. GIF files store a maximum of 256 colours and have a transparency feature that can make a specific colour transparent so that parts of an image do not obscure the one behind, as shown below.

Top Tip
Learn which of the file formats GIF and JPEG is lossy and which is lossless.

3. JPEG (Joint Photographic Expert Group)

This is a file format that uses lossy compression. Depending on the image, the loss of detail can be hardly noticeable or can seriously reduce the quality of the image.

Hardware required to display two-dimensional (2D) graphics

Displays

Large screens with a high resolution are required to produce the high-quality images needed for editing bit-mapped graphics and CAD (Computer-Aided Design).

Older computer systems used CRT (Cathode Ray Tube) monitors to display graphics. These were bulky and heavy and only suitable for desktop computers. Modern computer systems use either LCD or more expensive TFT flat screen displays.

Graphics card

A graphics card is a circuit board which manages the screen display for the computer system.

It has its own memory and processor to store and process the graphics data which takes pressure off the computer's main processor and memory.

Quick Test

1. Name two devices that are used to capture graphics for a computer system.

2. What does CCD stand for?

3. Which of these file formats uses lossy compression?

   A Bitmap   **B** JPEG   **C** GIF   **D** ASCII

4. What is the function of a graphics card?

Answers 1. Digital camera, scanner. **2.** Charge-Coupled Device. **3.** B **4.** A graphics card manages the screen display of the computer system.

Bit-mapped graphics data 2

Terms used in bit-mapped graphics

Resolution

The term 'resolution' is a measure of the size of the pixels in the image.

High-resolution graphics have a large number of small pixels.

Low-resolution graphics have a small number of large pixels.

High-resolution graphics have better quality than low-resolution graphics but require more storage.

Resolution is usually measured in dpi (dots per inch).

Colour depth

The colour depth is the number of bits used to store the colour of each pixel.

The higher the colour depth then the higher the number of colours that can be represented, thus improving the quality of an image.

The GIF file format has a colour depth of 8 bits, which gives a maximum of 256 colours.

The JPEG file format has a colour depth of 24 bits, which allows for over 16 million colours.

File size

Bit-mapped graphics have high storage requirements. Reducing the resolution, reducing the colour depth and lossy compression all contribute to smaller file sizes but at the expense of the quality of the image.

Top Tip

It is not specific enough to describe resolution as the quality of the image. Of course resolution has an influence on the quality of a graphic, but describe resolution in terms of the number and size of the pixels.

Bitmap editing software

The following tools and features are provided in bitmap editing software packages.

Paintbrush

The paintbrush tool allows a selected colour to be used to draw on the image with varying sizes of brush.

Fill

The fill tool allows a selected colour to be used to fill an area of an image.

Decrease resolution

Decreasing the resolution reduces the quality of the image, since there are fewer pixels but the file size is smaller.

Alter colour depth

Increasing the colour depth improves the quality of the image by increasing the number of colours, but at the cost of increasing the file size.

Alter brightness and contrast

Images that are too dark or too light can be improved by adjusting the brightness and contrast.

Re-size or scale

Scaling a graphic changes its size by enlarging or reducing.
The picture shown below has been enlarged and reduced.

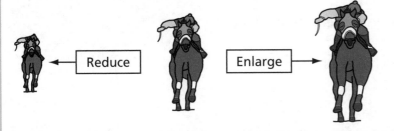

Reduce | Enlarge

Top Tip
Scaling an image doesn't just make it larger. When you scale an image, you can REDUCE or ENLARGE it.

Crop

Cropping a graphic means trimming its horizontal or vertical edges to show a particular area.

The picture shown has been cropped.

Crop →

Special effects

Bitmap editing software also provides special effects such as artistic effects, reflections, texture effects, etc.

Quick Test

1. Name a file format for graphics that uses lossless compression.
2. What effect does increasing the resolution of a bitmap graphic have on its file size?
3. What is the colour depth of a JPEG file?
4. What does it mean to crop an image?

Answers 1. GIF. 2. The file size will increase. 3. 24 bits. 4. Cropping means trimming the horizontal and vertical edges of an image.

Digitised sound data

Hardware required to capture sound data

Sound card

A sound card is a circuit board which manages the recording and playback of sound on a computer system.

The capturing of sound on a computer system requires a microphone and a sound card

The output of sound from a computer system requires a sound card and speakers.

Sound cards are also able to play music tracks on CDs and DVDs.

Top Tip

A sound card is similar to a graphics card, in that it has its own memory and processor to store and process the data, taking pressure off the computer's main processor and memory.

Storage of sound data

Sound data can be very large and so it is usually stored in compressed file formats. File formats for sounds can use both lossy and lossless compression.

The following are standard file formats for sounds:

1. RAW is an uncompressed file format.

2. WAV is a compressed file format which uses lossless compression.

3. MP3 is a compressed file format which uses lossy compression.

Top Tip

Standard file formats for sounds have been asked for several times in the exam, so learn each of their names and descriptions.

Terms used with sound data

Lossy compression

This reduces the file size but at the expense of quality. However, techniques such as removing sounds that are inaudible to the human ear can be applied so that the reduction in quality is hardly noticeable.

Sampling depth/resolution

This is the number of bits used to store a sample of sound. The higher the sampling depth the better the quality of the sound, since more bits are being used to describe the sound, but the file size is increased. Sampling depths of 8 bits and 16 bits are common.

Sampling frequency

This is the number of samples of the sound that are taken per second. The higher the sampling frequency the better the quality of the sound, since the sound is being sampled more often, but the file size is increased.

Sampling frequencies of 22 KHz (22,000 samples/sec) and 44 KHz (44,000 samples/sec) are common.

Sound time

This is the duration of the soundtrack measured in seconds. Long soundtracks can have a large file size.

Sound editing software

The following tools and features are provided in sound editing software packages.

Decrease sampling frequency

Decreasing the sampling frequency reduces the quality of the sound, since there are fewer samples taken per second, but the file size is smaller.

Decrease sampling depth

Decreasing the sampling depth reduces the quality of the sound by decreasing the number of bits used to store each sample, but the file size is smaller.

Crop

Cropping shortens the length of a track by cutting out parts of it.

Volume

The loudness of parts of a track or the loudness of individual instruments can be adjusted.

Reverse

Reversing means playing part of a track backwards.

Special effects

Sound editing software also provides special effects such as echoes, reverberation, etc.

Quick Test

1. What hardware is required to play a sound file?
2. Name a file format that uses lossless compression.
3. What unit is used to measure sampling frequency?
4. What does it mean to reverse a soundtrack?

Answers 1. A sound card and speakers. 2. WAV. 3. Hz or KHz. 4. To play a soundtrack backwards.

Video data

Hardware required to capture digital video data

Video is achieved on a computer system by showing a sequence of still frames. Digital video cameras and webcams are two input devices used to input video into a computer system.

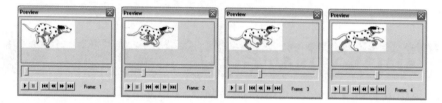

Digital video camera

High-quality video can be captured by a digital video camera. Settings such as colour depth, resolution and the number of frames captured per second can be used to control the quality of the video.

Webcam

A webcam can also be used to capture video for a computer system, but has poorer quality than a digital video camera.

Graphics card

A graphics card is required to input and output video data from a computer system. The graphics card is also used to compress and decompress video data.

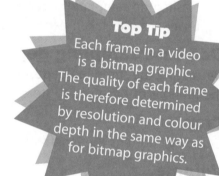

Top Tip
Each frame in a video is a bitmap graphic. The quality of each frame is therefore determined by resolution and colour depth in the same way as for bitmap graphics.

Storage of video data

Video data can be very large and so it is usually stored in compressed file formats.

The following are standard file formats for video:

1. AVI is an uncompressed file format.

2. MPEG is a compressed file format which uses lossy compression.

Terms used with video data

You are expected to know the meaning of the following terms and their effect on the quality of video.

Lossy compression
This removes data from the video file to reduce the file size but also reduces the quality of the video.

Colour depth (bytes)
Reducing the colour depth reduces the file size but also reduces the quality of the video, since fewer colours are represented.

Resolution
Reducing the resolution reduces the file size but also reduces the quality of the video since fewer pixels are used to represent each frame.

Frame rate (fps)
Reducing the frame rate reduces the file size but too low a frame rate can result in poor quality video which plays in a jerky movement.

Video time
This is the length of the video usually measured in seconds.

Video editing software

This software allows various means of editing video, including changing the sequence of clips, adding transition effects between clips, adding a soundtrack cropping, etc.

This course specifically requires you to know the term 'cropping' (or 'trimming'), which means: to cut out part of the video.

Top Tip
Investigate the features of the video editing software that you use in this course. Look into features such as frame rate, colour depth and cropping but also explore extra features not mentioned in this topic.

Quick Test

1. Name two devices that can be used to capture video for a computer system.

2. What is meant by the term 'frame rate'?

3. Name two standard file formats for video.

4. Apart from cropping, give another way of reducing the file size of video data.

Answers 1. Digital video camera, webcam, mobile phone, etc. 2. The number of frames per second (fps) 3. AVI and MPEG. 4. Reduce the resolution, colour depth or frame rate.

Vector graphics

Objects and attributes

Vector graphics store an image as a list of layered objects, each object being described by its attributes.

Attributes to describe a two-dimensional (2D) object include Shape, Position, Size, Line colour, Line thickness, Fill colour, Degree of rotation and Layer.

Three-dimensional (3D) images are described by similar attributes but also include additional attributes such as Texture and Shadow.

For example, the image shown was created in a vector graphics program.

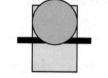

A vector graphics package does not store the colour of individual pixels but the objects and their attributes. In this example the Line, Circle and Rectangle objects would be stored as follows:

Object	Attributes
Line	start x, start y, end x, end y, line colour, line thickness, layer, etc.
Circle	centre x, centre y, radius, line colour, line thickness, fill colour, layer, etc.
Rectangle	start x, start y, length, breadth, line colour, line thickness, fill colour, layer, etc.

Features of vector graphics

File size

The file size of vector graphics is much smaller than for bitmap graphics, since only the objects and attributes need to be stored and not the colours of thousands or even millions of pixels.

Scalable

The objects in vector graphics can be enlarged without a reduction in quality, since the objects are described by their attributes and not the colours of individual pixels, as with bitmap graphics.

Editing

Vector graphics are edited at an object level by changing the attributes of objects so that objects can easily be moved, copied, re-sized, etc.

Layering

Vector graphics consist of a list of objects layered on top of each other.

The layer attribute of objects can be changed to bring objects to the front, sent back a layer, etc.

Top Tip
The ability to rescale vector graphics without loss of quality is called 'resolution independence'.

Top Tip
The drawing shapes in Microsoft Word are an example of vector graphics. Investigate attributes of these shapes such as fill colour, line thickness, layer, etc.

Common file formats

The following are standard file formats for vector graphics. These file formats allow the attributes of 2D and 3D objects to be stored.

1. SVG (Scalable Vector Graphics)

2. VRML (Virtual Reality Mark-up Language)

3. WRL (World Description Language)

Quick Test

1. In a vector graphics package which object is described by the following attributes?
start x, start y, end x, end y, line colour, line thickness, layer, etc.

2. Why is the eraser tool not found in a vector graphics package?

3. Why do vector graphics not become jagged and grainy when enlarged as with bitmap graphics?

4. Name a standard file format for vector graphics.

Answers 1. Line. **2.** An eraser tool is not found because individual pixels cannot be deleted; the image is edited by changing the attributes of objects, rather than deleting them. **3.** Vector graphics are resolution independent since the colours of the pixels themselves are not stored, just the objects and their attributes. **4.** SVG or VRML or WRL.

Synthesised sound and implications of multimedia technology

Synthesised sound

Synthesised sound is artificial sound produced by a computer system.

MIDI (musical instrument digital interface)

A MIDI interface is used to record synthesised music on a computer system. A MIDI instrument (usually a keyboard) is used to play the music, which can then be edited and played back.

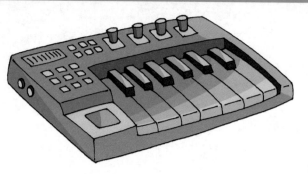

Each note of MIDI data is described by a list of attributes in a similar way to objects in a vector graphics program.

The following attributes are used to describe the notes stored in MIDI data:

1. **Instrument**

   A MIDI keyboard can produce different sounds to represent various instruments such as piano, violin, flute, etc. The instrument attribute specifies which of the instruments is to play the note.

2. **Pitch**

   This is the frequency of a note, or how high or low it is played.

3. **Volume**

   This attribute specifies how loudly or softly the note is played.

4. **Duration**

   This is the length of time the note lasts for.

5. **Tempo**

   MIDI music can be played back at different speeds. This attribute specifies the speed of the music.

Top Tip
The sounds produced by a MIDI keyboard are described by a limited number of attributes and so do not have the same complexity or detail as natural sound. For example, it will not produce a good representation of the human voice.

Top Tip
The music department in your school will almost certainly have a MIDI keyboard. Try to get the music teacher to give you a demonstration or an opportunity to try it out.

Implications of multimedia technology

Convergence of technology

The last decade has seen the increasing spread of hardware devices that combine two or more functions that used to be provided only by a single device.

The term 'convergence of technology' is used to describe a single device that provides two or more multimedia functions. For example, a smart phone can be used to send and receive calls, take pictures and video, access the Internet, play MP3 music, play video games, etc.

Other examples of convergence of technology are pocket PCs, digital television and virtual reality.

See also Unit 5: E-commerce and converging technologies, p. 66.)

Quick Test

1. What does MIDI stand for?

2. Why is a MIDI keyboard not good at synthesising a natural-sounding representation of the human voice?

3. Which of the following devices is not an example of convergence technology?

   A Mobile phone;   **B** Digital TV;   **C** Wireless keyboard;   **D** Pocket PC

4. What is meant by the term 'convergence of technology'?

Answers 1. Musical Instrument Digital Interface **2.** The human voice is too complex to be accurately described by the attributes of MIDI notes. **3.** C **4.** 'Convergence of technology' refers to two or more multimedia functions being provided in one device.

Test your progress

Questions

1. How are web pages created using a text editor?

2. What takes place at the maintenance stage of the software development process?

3. Which of the following would be an attribute of 3D vector graphics objects but not 2D objects?

    A Size;   **B** Rotation;   **C** Texture;   **D** Position

4. Which of these file formats uses lossless compression?

    A JPEG;   **B** Bitmap;   **C** ASCII;   **D** GIF

5. What units are used to measure resolution in a graphics package?

6. What is the effect of decreasing the colour depth of a bitmap graphic?

7. The music for a video game is created using a MIDI keyboard. Name two attributes of a MIDI note.

8. Apart from compression, give another way in which the size of a sound file can be reduced.

9. What effect would reducing the sampling frequency of a soundtrack have on quality?

10. Which effect does lossy compression have on the playing time of a video?

11. What feature of video editing software would be used to reduce a video which lasts for 12 to 10 minutes?

12. Which vector graphics attribute has been changed in the editing of Graphic A to Graphic B?

13. How is the graphic stored in a vector graphics package?

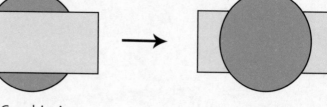

Graphic A   Graphic B

14. Wendy uses a presentation package to create a slide show for a History project at school. When she takes the file home it will not run on her own computer.

    Suggest why Wendy was unable to run the presentation.

15. Barry is the captain of his school's snooker team and wishes to produce a poster to attract new members to the snooker club. Bitmap editing software is used to create the poster. Part of the editing process is shown.

    Which tools have been used in the editing of Graphic A to Graphic B?

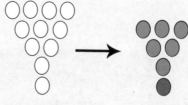

Graphic A   Graphic B

16. Winston is a teaching professional at Sun Valley Golf Club. He uses a digital video camera to take videos of members' golf swings. The videos are very jerky when played back.

    What can be done to the video recorder settings so that future videos are not so jerky?

Answers

1. HTML (Hypertext Mark-up Language) code is entered into the text editor.
2. The software is modified to remove previously undetected errors, add extra features and to adapt it to changes in the hardware or software environment.
3. C
4. D
5. Resolution is measured in dpi (dots per inch).
6. Decreasing the colour depth will reduce the quality of the image and the file size will be smaller.
7. Any two from instrument, pitch, volume, duration and tempo.
8. Reducing the sampling depth, sampling frequency or sound time.
9. The sound would be of poorer quality.
10. None.
11. Cropping/trimming.
12. Layer.
13. The graphic is stored as a list of layered objects and their attributes.
14. Wendy did not have the application package or player to run the file.
15. Fill and crop tools.
16. The frame rate setting can be increased.

How did you score

Number of answers correct:

0–6 Not very good. You need to go back and learn this topic.

7–9 Reasonable. You know some of the work but look over before moving on.

10–13 Good. You should move on but go back later and consolidate your knowledge.

14–16 Excellent. You have mastered this topic and can move on.

Overview and hints

Introduction

A new coursework task is published every year to prevent candidates from cheating, and usually comes out around the beginning of November.

The task is designed to test your ability to apply knowledge, understanding and practical abilities that you have developed in the Computer Systems and Software Development units.

The optional units are not assessed in the coursework task.

Top Tip
Talk to pupils in your school who did this course last year and ask them for any advice on how to go about the coursework task.

Overview

1. The coursework task is worth 30 marks and the written exam is worth 70 marks.

2. There is a time allocation of between 8 and 10 hours, although this can be extended at the discretion of your teacher. Marks could be deducted if you take far too long.

3. The task is carried out under 'open book' conditions under the supervision of your teacher, to ensure that the work you submit is your own.

4. The task always has one part based on the Computer Systems unit and one part based on the Software Development unit. Each part is worth 15 marks.

5. Your teacher will give you the specification of the task and the marking scheme.

6. If you are stuck you can seek help from your teacher, but marks will be deducted to reflect the amount of help given.

7. Unlike NAB assessments, you do not need to pass the coursework task to pass the course, but obviously it will not help your overall grade if you fail.

8. Your performance in the coursework task, combined with your prelim exam performance, should be used by your school to estimate your grade for the course.

Hints

There are measures that you can take to prepare yourself for the coursework task before it is given out by your teacher.

1. Use the Internet and computer magazines to keep up-to-date with hardware devices and their specification and cost.

2. Thoroughly study the topics 'Types of computer and performance', 'Peripherals 1' and 'Peripherals 2' in the 'Computer systems' unit.

3. Make sure that you can represent a program algorithm using pseudocode, because you will be asked to do this in the task.

4. Know what you are expected to do to test a program using test data.

5. Get as much practice as possible in the programming language that you use before you start the coursework task.

6. The actual program implementation will require aspects of programming such as selecting correct variable types, 'if' statements, loops and validating entered data.

7. Make sure that you use meaningful variable names, internal commentary and indents and blank lines to make your program readable and give it structure.

8. Make sure that your report for the task is complete, neat and well presented.

Top Tip
Get hold of the coursework tasks for previous years. There are patterns in what is asked for each year and it will help to prepare you for what to expect and to be more confident.

Index